food Wales
a second helping

GRAFFEG

Published by Graffeg
First published 2005
Second edition published 2008
Copyright © Graffeg 2005, 2008
ISBN 9781905582150

Graffeg,
Radnor Court,
256 Cowbridge Road East,
Cardiff CF5 1GZ Wales UK.
T: +44 (0)29 2037 7312
sales@graffeg.com
www.graffeg.com

Distributed by the Welsh Books
Council www.cllc.org.uk
castellbrychan@cllc.org.uk

A CIP Catalogue record for this
book is available from the British
Library.

Designed and produced by
Peter Gill & Associates
sales@petergill.com
www.petergill.com

Food Wales written by
Colin Pressdee.

Thanks to Carwyn Evans for
undertaking much research
and assisting in compiling the
contents.

Every effort has been made to
ensure that the information in this
book is current and it is given
in good faith at the time of
publication. Please be aware that
circumstances can change and
be sure to check details before
visiting any of the restaurants
featured.

Picture credits:
Alamy: © Arco Images GmbH: 134 / © Guichaoua: 134 /
© Bobbie Lerryn: 134. © britainonview / Andy Stothert:
46, 48 / British Tourist Authority: 72, 113, 126 / Derek
Forss: 21 / Graham Bell: 76, 78 / James Osmond: 10
/ Jeff Morgan: 112 / NTPL / Joe Cornish: 74 / Tom
McGahan: 38, 158. © Anthony Blake Photolibrary:
52, 94. © Crown copyright (2008) Food and Marketing
Development Division: 4, 6, 7, 16, 20, 22, 24, 28, 30, 34,
35, 37, 38, 40, 46, 49, 50, 52, 54, 55, 56, 57, 58, 60, 61,
63, 64, 65, 66, 67, 69, 76, 77, 78, 80, 82, 84, 86, 88, 92,
94, 96, 99, 101, 102, 110, 114, 116, 117, 118, 120, 122,
123, 126, 136, 152, 166, 179, 180. © Crown copyright
(2008) Visit Wales: 12, 14, 30, 48, 60, 64, 82, 110.
© David Williams: 34, 108, 110. © Harry Williams: 4, 16,
32, 80, 160. © Imagephotographic.co.uk: 135, 165, 166,
172, 174, 177, 183. © Mansel Davies: 82, 153.
© Monddi: 104. © Peter Gill & Associates: 117, 167,
184. © Photolibrary Wales: 12, 52, 86, 124.
© Really Welsh Trading Company: 114. © StockFood.
com: Euler, Bernd: 74 / Finley, Marc O: 152 / Fisher,
Tara: 24 / Foodcollection: 18 / FoodFoto Kˆln: 94 / Rees,
Peter: 162 / Schindler, Martina: 180.
Inside back cover: © StockFood.com: Cazals, Jean /
Leser, Nicolas / Bischoff, Harry / Fisher, Tara / King,
Dave. © Aber / Alamy. © Harry Williams.

food
Wales
a second helping

A second culinary journey with Colin Pressdee
- where to find, taste and buy the best local,
seasonal, natural and sustainable foods in Wales.

GRAFFEG

Contents

introduction

Harvesting the seashore in the Burry Estuary – Whitford Point lighthouse is in the distance.

more sustainable fishing techniques ensure that we are conserving stocks, which is vitally important for the future

local produce features on menus from bar meals to banquets

In the three years since the first edition of Food Wales was published, the Welsh food industry has gathered considerable momentum.

Wales' organic sector has grown remarkably with 710 Welsh companies in 2006 listed as organic and occupying 7878,973 hectares of land. Beef and sheep production dominate organic farming in Wales, and as a consequence 81% of fully organic land is permanent grassland. We have also seen a significant development in primary production, particularly in the dairy industry, led by dedicated Welsh producers and rising consumer demand.

Across the country more producers have formed groups able to market their collective products more effectively. Local authorities have set up departments dedicated to helping companies to package and market their products more efficiently, enabling appearances at major food exhibitions and conventions in Britain and Europe. The catering industry has grown across the board. From luxury country house hotels to rural and urban restaurants and public houses, the quality and scope of the offering is far broader, with local produce featuring on more menus from bar meals to banquets.

Local food is more readily available from an increasing number of farm shops specialising in their own and the area's produce. Regular farmers' markets are held in almost every town and village in Wales, and the variety of produce available has expanded from just meat and vegetables to include dairy and bakery products, cooked meats, pâtés, preserves and a wide range of artisan food.

The nation's annual calendar of food festivals now runs from Easter until Christmas with most weekends covered throughout the season. The scope of these events ranges from an extended farmers' market right up to a full-blown programme of celebrity chef demonstrations and debates on how the industry should develop. Some of these festivals, particularly the Abergavenny Food Festival in September, attract UK-wide publicity.

Local food is more readily available from an increasing number of farm shops specialising in their own and the area's produce.

Food Wales – a second helping, highlights regional foods

About this book

In each section this book highlights the primary producers and food-related businesses that utilise Wales' natural resources, as well as those with intrinsic Welsh values and those that use traditional Welsh recipes and ingredients in their production process.

Food producers

The food producers listed range from small artisan workshops up to large-scale manufacturers that utilise local resources. Some of their fare might only be available in small local markets, farm shops, town and village stores, while the rest will be more widely available in larger outlets and multiples. Many of these businesses are reaching broad markets via their websites and supplying nationally by mail order and overnight delivery.

Seasonality

Thankfully in recent years there has been a return to seasonality. More caterers are using produce in its natural season rather than trying to keep a false menu going throughout the year using imported and frozen goods. This has led to more interesting menus being offered in establishments across Wales from simple tearooms to top hotels and restaurants. The quality of food now served in many restaurants is as high as other areas of Britain and compares favourably to some of the best in major cities.

Where to eat

In each region the book lists, as far as possible, the restaurants, pubs, hotels, caterers and cafés that aim to utilise quality local Welsh seasonal produce – the definition of 'local' in most places being produce purchased directly from suppliers as opposed to the local supermarket, or supplies received via a local van delivery service. The level of culinary skill varies, but at every level the best examples of those in sympathy with the local produce are listed.

Regional Welsh foods

The increase in awareness of the fine produce of Wales, as well as other countries that produce distinctive regional food, has led to a revival of fine food retailing outlets and quality delicatessens that are flourishing alongside the multiples. This trend has forced the multiples to look themselves at stocking regional foods and there has been a marked increase in listings within Wales of regional Welsh foods.

There are now distinctive sections of the community that will shop in local markets, farm shops and delicatessens knowing that the cost of quality is well worth the extra money. And there is now a definite choice in the market between mass-produced food – whether poultry, meat, vegetables and dairy products – and smaller scale, quality, seasonal organic produce and true artisan foods.

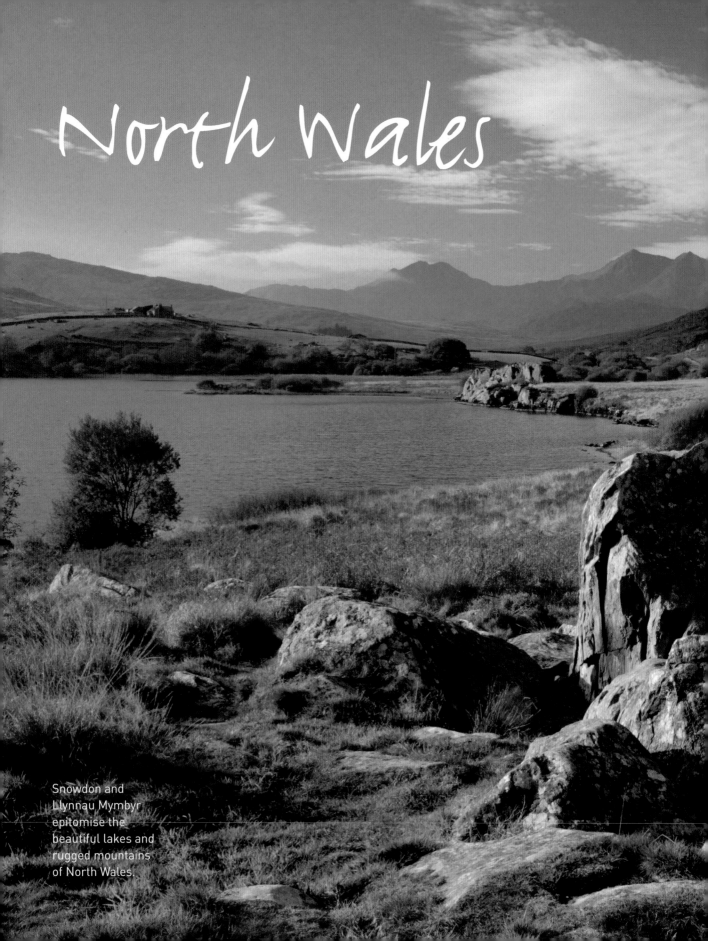

North Wales

Snowdon and
Llynnau Mymbyr
epitomise the
beautiful lakes and
rugged mountains
of North Wales.

North Wales

This land extends from Bardsey Island to the Dee Estuary, the Isle of Anglesey to the River Dyfi and Berwyn Mountains. The mighty mountains, mirror lakes and torrent rivers of Snowdonia, the rugged Llŷn coastline, sandy bays, and green pastures of the vales of Dee and Clwyd, produce as diverse as the area. Aberdaron lobster, Bangor mussels, Anglesey beef and Snowdonia lamb make a low-food-miles menu second to none.

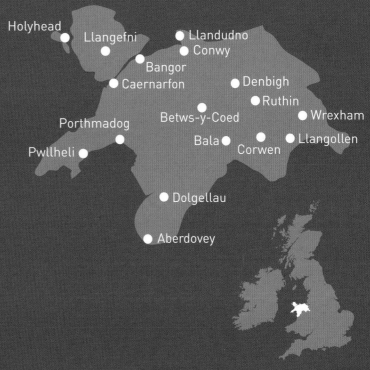

Holyhead
Llangefni
Llandudno
Conwy
Bangor
Caernarfon
Denbigh
Ruthin
Betws-y-Coed
Wrexham
Porthmadog
Bala
Llangollen
Corwen
Pwllheli
Dolgellau
Aberdovey

North Wales: about the area

Nant Gwynant is one of many glacial valleys in Snowdonia. The waterfall is one of many where the river tumbles from the lofty heights of Snowdonia.

This large area extends from the Llŷn Peninsula and Bardsey Island in the west almost to Chester. Its southern regions include the Dyfi Estuary, the Dee Valley and the Berwyn mountains; to the north lie Anglesey, Conwy and Flintshire, and north to the Isle of Anglesey. It takes in the mountain peaks of Snowdonia, the rolling pastures of Denbighshire through to the low-lying border country.

The coastline extends from the sweeping beaches of Cardigan Bay with large river estuaries and salt marsh plains, to the wild and rugged Llŷn Peninsula, the dramatic flowing Menai Straits and gentler Liverpool Bay.

The entire area is dissected by numerous rivers flowing from Snowdonia and the Berwyns. Glaslyn, Mawddach and Dyfi are true torrent rivers flowing into Cardigan Bay. The Conwy cuts its way from the mountains directly northwards to the coast, while the Dee flows from Lake Bala through the Vale of Llangollen meandering its way along the borderlands to the sea beyond Chester.

Snowdonia

Snowdonia is defined by the area of the National Park that stretches from the Dyfi Estuary to the Conwy Valley and almost to the Menai Straits. The massive mountainous area was shaped by the Ice Age that carved out the main features of deep glacial valleys, mountain cwms and the sheer precipices and screes of the mountains. A classic view is from the A487 descending towards Tal-y-Llyn. The U-shaped valley and the natural lake make a postcard photograph. Another stunning view is from Nantlle and the scene captured by Richard Wilson on his famous mountainscape of Snowdonia. Mountaineers have the privilege of the fabulous sights such as Llŷn Cau close to the summit of Cadair Idris.

Llŷn Peninsula

The Llŷn Peninsula stretches 30 miles west into the Irish Sea from the Menai Straits to the remote Island of Bardsey. The dramatic view of Bardsey Sound reminds us of the treacherous journey taken by the numerous pilgrims who sought sanctuary at St Mary's Abbey. The north of the area is dominated by mountains that rise sharply from the sea to over 500 metres at Gyrn Ddu, Bwlch Mawr and Yr Eifl. The coastline west of Trefor is steep and rugged in many areas showing evidence of the granite quarrying that flourished in the nineteenth century. To the south sandy bays at Abersôch, Pwllheli and Criccieth are popular beach resorts with sailing, boating and fishing attracting many visitors. Porth Neigwl or Hell's Mouth is one of the most renowned surfing beaches with four miles of sand frequently battered by white-crested breakers.

Anglesey

The Isle of Anglesey is covered with prehistoric fortresses, earthworks and burial chambers. It has evidence of human habitation from Neolithic times with burial chambers at Bryn Celli Ddu, Bodowyr, Lligwy, and Barclodiad y Gawres and numerous others. Holyhead has been a seaport for Ireland since the Romans established a fortress in the sheltered north of Holy Island. It developed in the Victorian era when Anglesey was linked to the mainland by the two famous bridges. The Menai Suspension Bridge was built by Thomas Telford opened in 1826 and Stevenson's Britannia Bridge was completed in 1850 but was destroyed by fire in 1970 and replaced with the present structure. Holyhead is still the busiest port for the Irish ferries.

Amlwch on the northern coast was the centre of the copper industry exporting worldwide. The sheltered harbour is now used by fishing boats and leisure craft. Beaumaris was established by Edward I as his fortress guarding the entrance to the

The sun sets over Cemaes Bay, an Area of Outstanding Natural Beauty and the most northerly village in Wales.

Menai Straits. It developed in the middle ages and became a popular destination in Victorian times. The central market town of Llangefni was renowned for its livestock market. The quality of Anglesey's cattle and sheep has been proven by many supreme champions in the Royal Smithfield and Royal Welsh agricultural shows.

Uplands

The land east of the Conwy Valley takes in the uplands of Mynydd Hiraethog, the Clwydian Range, the Horseshoe Pass and south to the Berwyn Mountains that rise to 800 metres. Much of the upland heath is around 500 metres and extends from east of Llanrwst to Mold, dissected by many small river valleys and the main Vale of Clwyd. To the south is the Dee Valley from Lake Bala to Llangollen where it tumbles through the town, after which it meanders its way through the county of Wrexham to the sea beyond Chester.

Industry

In the past the North Wales area attracted heavy industry with coal mining and steel making around Wrexham. Today, the region has achieved success in attracting new and highly skilled industries, especially to the business and technology parks of Wrexham and Flintshire. Wales's largest industrial site is Airbus UK at Broughton, where the wings for the enormous Airbus A380 aircraft are made. Quarrying granite on the cliffs of the north Llŷn around to Penmaenmawr and Abergele was very active up to the early twentieth century. Slate mining shows its evidence in many areas, particularly at Corris, Blaenau Ffestiniog, the Horseshoe Pass and Nantlle. The main active slate exploitation is at Bethesda on the precipitous terraces of a massive quarry.

In the last 40 years forestry has been a major business in many areas shrouding the natural beauty of the landscape with regimented rows of fir trees. The quick growth of these trees gives a timber crop several times each generation compared to the slow return on indigenous trees.

New to the landscape are wind turbines that produce green electricity while they blight the skyline of many of the most stunning mountainous areas. Less visible are hydro-electric stations that harness the power of water tumbling from reservoirs high in the mountains.

Despite the activity and previous exploitation most of the landscape and coastal features are remarkably untarnished. The beauty of Snowdonia with its precipitous crags and Welsh cwms, white torrent rivers, heather-topped hills and azure mountain lakes remains stunning. It attracts numerous mountain walkers and adventurers of all kinds.

Population

The sparsely populated area has many small villages originally sited on drovers' trails. Larger towns grew from the Norman fortifications and the great castles around the coast, particularly at Harlech, Caernarfon, Conwy and Beaumaris. Over the centuries these towns retained their importance as local administration centres, attracting commerce, businesses and the associated professions.

Former fishing villages have developed into holiday resorts, particularly on Anglesey and the Llŷn Peninsula.

The towns of Porthmadog, Pwllheli, Abersôch, Caernarfon, Conwy and Beaumaris have new marinas and water sports centres that attract sailing and other leisure activities. Some of the sheltered coastal areas that developed into resorts during the Victorian area have remained popular. Recent heavy investment in a considerable number of hotels has brought new-money prosperity, revitalising hitherto declining areas.

Most of the main urban centres of the area are market towns. Llangefni on Anglesey, Denbigh, Llangollen, Corwen and Ruthin have their heart in the agricultural heritage of the area even though things have changed more recently. Some of the livestock markets have gone, but they have been superseded by weekend craft, food and rural goods markets.

Tourists

Tourism is an important industry in North Wales. The area has numerous attractions in its natural beauty, added to by some innovation over the years. The Snowdonia Mountain Railway is one of the best examples of a development that has enhanced enjoyment of an area without destroying any of its beauty. From a different origin the Ffestiniog railway from Porthmadog that used to bring slate from Blaenau Ffestiniog for export is now a major tourist attraction sitting well into the landscape.

White water rafting and canoeing at Tryweryn and Llangollen uses the natural elements to provide the most exciting sport. Many people get their kicks from the challenging mountaineering throughout the Snowdonia range, and the triumph of reaching a summit with its spectacular views is truly exhilarating. Mountain walking and biking are hugely popular and generally very safe pursuits.

The coastline provides a whole host of experiences for sportsmen and women. Boating, fishing, sailing, surfing and swimming are popular in many areas. There are renowned links golf courses at Aberdyfi, Harlech, Nefyn, Holyhead and Conwy – favoured by locals and visitors – and major competitions are staged.

Rivers

The main rivers still have stocks of salmon and sewin (sea trout) in the migration season. The Dyfi, Mawddach, Glaslyn, Seiont, Conwy and Dee have many miles of renowned beats that bring many anglers to the area. Lakes and reservoirs are well

Many restaurants cook using locally sourced produce including a variety of greens.

Tyddyn Llan Restaurant with Rooms was voted the Good Food Guide's Wales restaurant of the year in 2007 and 2008.

Mackerel are fished in the waters surrounding North Wales. They are best enjoyed at their freshest.

T J Roberts & Son is a traditional butcher in Bala with locally sourced and well-hung Welsh Black beef, pork and lamb.

stocked with natural brown trout and rainbow trout that provide excellent sport. The natural Lake Tal-y-Llŷn in the shadow of Cadair Idris is one of the most renowned for brown trout and also salmon during the season. Many of the mountain lakes in corries hold char that date back to the Ice Age when these lakes were carved into the landscape. Similarly Lake Bala has an unusual species, the gwyniad, a type of trout that is very elusive to most anglers.

Land

The nature of the land lends itself more to livestock production than arable farming. The uplands of Snowdonia, Cadair Idris and Llŷn Peninsula are vast areas for grazing sheep in the summer when growth of heather and wild herbs, flowers and grass give plentiful feed. In winter stocks are moved to lower ground to avoid inhospitable conditions. The lower hinterland, Denbigh and the Isle of Anglesey in particular are well renowned for cattle for dairy production and meat. The lush rolling pastures are watered regularly but not with the violence of the torrential rainfall of Snowdonia.
Areas in the rain shadow of the mountains extend from Anglesey and across the mainland to the vale of Clwyd and Dee. In these areas there is combination of traditional mixed agriculture and larger scale beef and dairy farms. The upland moors extend over vast areas and make suitable summer grazing for sheep. These were once renowned for wild red grouse and efforts are planned to reintroduce this bird for its sporting potential.
North Wales has the most diverse terrain of anywhere in Wales or south of Scotland. It certainly has some of the wildest countryside imaginable from the heights of Snowdonia with its deep valleys to the wave battered exposed coastline west of the Llŷn. There are many areas of sheltered bays and gentle pastures in the

shadow of towering mountain ranges. It has become the major tourism destination area for the sheer diversity of outdoor pursuits.

Food

The food industry is highly developed in this area with a number of substantial companies in large scale production for the multiple and food service industries, plus medium and small scale units, and many artisan companies. Much of the production is linked to the meat and dairy industries, with several substantial organic producers. The number of good quality food shops has increased in recent years, with some notable farm shops and farmers' markets. The sparsely spread population in most areas but for the North East, the coastal strip, parts of the Llŷn and the Dyfi Estuary hardly creates demand for food shops comparable to that in the larger towns of Conwy and Pwllheli.

The catering and hospitality industry has developed to meet the demands and aspirations of the twenty-first century market. Two decades ago it was still dubbed a gastronomic desert, but now there are numerous luxury country house hotels, gourmet restaurants, resort hotels of quality and gastro pubs catering for sophisticated clientele. The proximity to the conurbations of Manchester, Liverpool, Cheshire and the West Midlands brings numerous people seeking short breaks and overnight stays who expect the quality commensurate with major cities.

North Wales: food of the area

Spider crabs are caught in lobster pots from the coastal waters of Llŷn and Anglesey.

Halen Môn's increasingly famous white crystals can be found in Marks and Spencer, Waitrose and Harvey Nichols as well as in the kitchens of top restaurants world-wide.

Mussels

The long coastline from the Dyfi to the Dee, taking in the Llŷn Peninsula and Anglesey has considerable resources that have been fished and harvested since earliest times. The estuaries, inter-tidal and coastal waters and offshore deep waters have been a source of fish and shellfish producing considerable income for small and large operators, and associated marketing and processing businesses.

Through history the mussel beds of Conwy, Porthmadog, Bangor and the Menai Straits have provided an important source of food and income. The current fisheries are based at Conwy, Brynsiencyn and Port Penrhyn, the latter being the largest fishery in Britain harvesting up to 15,000 tons annually, mostly for export. The former have purification plants and supply the local and national markets. Both Conwy and Anglesey mussels feature on many restaurant menus and in retail shops.

Fishing

Lobster and crab fishing using traditional creels around the coastal waters of the Llŷn and Anglesey takes place from spring to late autumn. Small fleets operate from Aberdaron, Abersoch, Holyhead, Amlwch, Conwy and numerous small harbours. Most of the catch is exported live in vivier lorries (with sea water tanks) to the lucrative markets in France and Spain. Processing crab meat provides a good income for several small operators.

Small fleets of trawlers fish with otter and beam trawls for prime species such as sole, plaice, turbot, brill and skate. Some larger boats are equipped to dredge scallops, particularly from Holyhead. Many also line fish for bass, mackerel, cod and mullet. The Llŷn Fishermens' Co-operative is based at Pwllheli and assists in co-ordinating the marketing and processing of landings. Several companies market the catch locally and throughout Wales and the Midlands putting Llŷn fish on many restaurant menus.

The Menai Straits has the only oyster fishery in Wales producing the Pacific rock oyster by laying oyster spat (seed) in nets to grow on to market size. They are purified along with mussels at a processing plant near Brynsiencyn and distributed to specialists throughout the country.

One of the oldest fish farm in Britain is Chirk Trout Farm at Glyn Ceiriog, still in operation after 100 years. They produce brown and rainbow trout both for the table and re-stocking lakes and reservoirs for angling. The plentiful pure water that tumbles from the Berwyns supplies the farm even in the driest of summers. New is the Blue Water Flatfish farm on Anglesey in an old quarry that links to the sea near Moelfre. Turbot, the most highly prized flatfish, are farmed to market size weighing about a kilo each.

Smoked fish and sea salt

A traditional corollary of the fishing industry is curing and smoking the catch. The herring curing sheds lie empty on Nefyn beach, but several excellent companies smoke fish and other products on Anglesey and at Llandudno. Another interesting development from fishing is the Sea Zoo at Brynsiencyn which is now a major tourist attraction. From this grew the unique Anglesey Sea Salt Company that extracts purest, organically certified sea salt from the local waters and markets it under the internationally known brand Halen Môn.

Agriculture

The massive land area produces a very wide range of foods that are reared, cultivated and foraged. The mountainous areas of Cadair Idris, Snowdonia and the Berwyns can be most inhospitable in winter, but are used for summer grazing producing most distinctive mountain lamb. A producer group the Snowdonia Mountain Lamb Society has very successfully marketed this lamb throughout Britain. The estuaries of the

Dyfi, Mawddach, Glaslyn, Conwy and Dee, plus coastal areas that flood on the equinox spring tides on the Llŷn produce salt marsh lamb throughout the summer and autumn. This too is becoming a very sought after speciality food in prime markets.

Lamb comes from all areas of North Wales and specific marketing has shown to be very effective as the producers of Elwy Valley Lamb have shown. This is now a distinctive name on many menus of top restaurants throughout London and the rest of the UK.

Beef and dairy farming is very important throughout the area on lower land particularly on the Llŷn, Anglesey, Vale of Clwyd and the Dee Valley. There has been a revival of the traditional Welsh Black as an important breed for its quality meat. The gentle pastures of Anglesey are particularly well known for top quality beef production.

Some very fine blue cheeses such as Gorau Glas are mild, creamy and delicious.

Dairy

Dairy farming is equally important in the mixed agricultural economy. A most successful producer group is the co-operative of South Caernarfon Creameries. They process milk, cheese and butter, with well known brands including Hen Sir (Old Shire), recognised as one of the finest large scale production cheddar cheeses.

Organic

Organic farming throughout Wales is increasing significantly. One of the leaders is the Rhug Organic Estate near Corwen in the Dee Valley. This covers 12,000 acres of land from the river valley to the Berwyn Mountains, taking in much pasture, arable land, forest and upland. It produces everything under the organic standards of the Soil Association including Welsh lamb, chickens, turkeys for Christmas, Aberdeen Angus pedigree beef. Duroc pork comes from their other organic estate in Shropshire. Salt marsh lamb comes from their Llŷn farm currently under conversion to organic. The produce is distributed nationally and available in their farm shop and from the website.

Vegetables

Vegetables and fruit are produced by many farms particularly along the more sunny northern coast in the rain shadow of Snowdonia. Parts of Anglesey have mixed farms and agriculture, some specialising in fruit for the pick-your-own summer trade.

Woodlands O'r Coed

Sustainability is a word that is heard increasingly throughout food production at every level. A flagship project O'r Coed was undertaken in 2006-7 in the county of Wrexham. The area actually covers very mixed terrain from the Berwyn Mountains, Ceiriog Valley, Llandegla Moors and the Dee Valley from Llangollen to the sea beyond Chester. It takes in a large amount of

Herding sheep in Trefriw, Conwy, Wales.

former and present woodland. The project aimed to cover the sustainable use of all woodland produce of the area including timber, wool, plants for artisan crafts, wild food and traditionally produced farm food. The project demonstrated the wide range of produce available in this area, much of which is totally under-utilised.

Game

A wide selection of wild game is very plentiful throughout the entire area of North Wales. Large estates rear venison and pheasants and there are significant amounts of wild stock of both. Estuaries are home to wild water fowl including ducks and geese, particularly in winter months. Woodcock and snipe are highly prized yet plentiful at this time. Hare, rabbit and pigeon all increase the bags of the organised estate shoots for pheasant and partridge. Some of the mountain heaths used to have wild red grouse population

and attempts are in hand to re-introduce this prized species. Wild black grouse do inhabit some forests but unfortunately are very rare.

Food processing

Food processing and manufacturing have become increasingly important in the last decade. The entire range of primary production has the possibility of a value added element that can increase revenue and employment in the area of production. This applies equally to seafood as to meat, vegetables and dairy produce.

Demand

The food market in Britain has become increasingly sophisticated, creating a strong demand for speciality produce, as well as the mass produced. This has led to a large number of small and medium sized companies finding their niche in these markets. Alongside this

 RED WINE
~ SPECIAL ~
FINCA EL
RETIRO
MALBEC
2001 £12·50

 GOATS
CHEESE SALAD
WITH SUN DRIED
TOMATOES +
OLIVES £5·25

WHITE WINE
SPECIAL
~ SPECIAL ~
LES GROGNOTS
BOURGOGNE

SMOKED
TROUT HOT POT
WITH FENNEL,
CREAM,

Patchwork Traditional Food Company use the finest ingredients to create their award-winning pates.

The mild climate enables a variety of tomatoes to be grown.

Hot oak-smoked salmon, one of the many innovative smoked specialities from the Derimôn Smokery.

some of the established companies have seen significant growth in the market particularly for packaged and ready made foods for the multiples and the food service industry.

Speciality foods

The speciality market is served by many companies in various market segments. Prepared, smoked and cured seafoods come from companies such as Llŷn Seafoods, Selective Seafoods, Derimôn Smokery and the Llandudno Smokery.

Dairy products of note come from The Village Dairy (Llaeth y Llan), and include the award-winning blue cheese from Gorau Glas on Anglesey. One of the biggest in the speciality market is Patchwork Traditional Foods, makers of a range of pâtés, flans and pies. These are seen in almost every independent delicatessen throughout the UK.

The market for speciality pies has grown immensely in the last few years. Harvies Pies of Nercwys produce a range from Welsh Black beef, organic beef and lamb, plus fish, cheese and vegetables, which are on sale in top London stores as well as local shops. The notable butcher Edwards of Conwy is renowned for quality handmade pies and sausages as well as top quality meat. Sausages are now produced by their associated Welsh Sausages Company of Conwy where they are branded packaged and distributed throughout Britain to major outlets and multiples.

The food service industry has expanded rapidly in the last decade and some leaders have performed well in this sector.

Roberts of Port Dinorwic are well established suppliers of cooked meats and ready made meals and have expanded significantly as this market has grown. Similarly KK Finefoods of Flint who were specialists in the vegetarian market have extended their new premises further to accommodate the latest technology to cater for the whole range of foods to this market.

Drink

The drinks market relies on the purest water which is in plentiful supply – some areas of Snowdonia receive over 100 inches of rain each year.

The bottled water market has grown exponentially, something inconceivable a generation ago. Decantae Mineral Water has placed itself at the premium end of the market with stylish bottles destined for top restaurants. Similarly the premium bottled beer market has led to the establishment of many small breweries making distinctive beer.

The Conwy Brewery has a range of about 10 beers. Bragdy Ynys Môn – has a similar range with its own distinctive style. The Great Orme Brewery also produces cask conditioned ales for local distribution. It seems a shame that Wales' distinctive Wrexham Lager has not been revived.

Though this area is at the northern extreme for vineyards, experiments have shown that – in certain places, with micro-climates that capture plenty of sun – it is possible to produce ripe grapes.

Another answer is employed by Worthenbury Wines of Gresford in the Dee Valley. They grow vines in poly tunnels to assist with the ripening of varieties such as Chardonnay, Sauvignon and Merlot. Though the EU vineyard rules prohibit this method of viticulture the result is surprisingly good wine with quite distinctive varietal character. It is sold locally in retailers and farmers' markets.

North Wales: where to eat

Rock oysters grow superbly in the clean waters of the Menai Straits.

Magnificent gardens of the stunning Bodysgallen Hall.

The high tide virtually laps the terrace of the row of former fishermen's cottages, now the Ship Inn in Red Wharf Bay, Anglesey.

56 The High Street, Mold

Set between shops this neat restaurant has light, contemporary décor and a menu from local Welsh foods. Fish from the coast include mussels, mullet, monkfish and lobster with Welsh lamb, beef and cheeses presented in stylish dishes at a reasonable cost. Friendly service and inexpensive wines make this a great addition to this old market town.
56 High Street, Mold CH7 1BD
T: 01352 759225

Amser Da, Llanrwst

Expect a panoply of Welsh produce and home baked foods in this bustling town bistro, with plenty of wines at friendly prices.
34 Heol Yr Orsaf, Llanrwst LL26 0BT
T: 01492 641188

Bay Leaf Bistro, Colwyn Bay

This small, neat bistro serves well-prepared, tasty dishes, many of which are inspired by locally sourced foods.
124 Abergele Road, Colwyn Bay LL29 7PS
T: 01492 531555

Bistro, Conwy

The church-hall-like exterior belies the warmth of ambience inside. Enthusiastic young staff present a menu that sings of local Welsh produce in some traditional and novel modern dishes. The cooking is highly competent. Expect Conwy mussels, fresh fish, Welsh Black beef, slow cooked duck and the house special local lamb that all come in generous portions at very fair prices.
Chapel Street, Conwy LL32 8BP
T: 01492 596326
www.bistroconwy.com

Bistro on the Square, Aberdyfi

Relaxed bistro with wonderful home cooking from prime ingredients at reasonable prices.
1 Chapel Square, Aberdyfi LL35 0EL
T: 01654 767448

The Boat Inn, Erbistock

A delightful setting on the lower River Dee, with a pub and restaurant menu and function facilities.
Erbistock, Wrexham LL13 0DL
T: 01978 780666

Boathouse, Holyhead

Fresh seafoods landed by local boats feature regularly on the menu.
Newry beach, Holyhead, Anglesey LL65 1YF
T: 01407 762094
E: boathousehotel@supanet.com
www.boathouse-hotel.co.uk

Bodysgallen Hall and Spa, Llandudno

Expect top quality country house hotel cooking in contemporary style at this magnificent seventeenth century manor. Finely judged cooking at all levels include local seafood and grand cuisine ingredients across to vegetables, salad and cheese. Service is formal but knowledgeable and attentive. Superb rooms, public areas, garden and spa.
Pentywyn Road, Llandudno LL30 1RS
T: 01492 584466
E: info@bodysgallen.com
www.bodysgallen.com

Bridge Inn, Menai Bridge

Pub wine bar with tasty bistro food in bar and conservatory.
Telford Road, Menai Bridge LL59 5DT
T: 01248 716888

Bryn Tyrch Hotel, Capel Curig

Hearty food with good vegetarian dishes, popular with mountain ramblers.
Capel Curig, Betws-y-Coed LL24 0EL
T: 01690 720223

Bull, Llangefni

Traditional pub with fine Anglesey meat served generously.
Bulkley Square, Llangefni, Anglesey LL77 7LR
T: 01248 722119

Caban Café, Brynrefail

All day café with Welsh and cosmopolitan dishes.
Yr Hen Ysgol, Brynrefail, Llanberis LL55 3NR
T: 01286 685500 E: caban@caban-cyf.org
www.caban-cyf.org

Café Neptune, Beaumaris

This modern first floor restaurant has an innovative design depicting an aquatic theme. This runs through the food with copious local seafood including Menai mussels and oysters. Freshest bass, mullet and turbot and other species in season are treated simply or with spicy sauces. Welsh Black beef and local lamb and tasty original desserts complete a generous offering.
First floor, 27 Castle Street, Beaumaris, Anglesey LL58 8AP
T: 01248 812990

Castell Deudraeth, Portmeirion

This beautifully appointed converted folly castle has superb rooms. The modern restaurant serves local food in brasserie style.
Portmeirion LL48 6EN
T: 01766 772400
E: castell@portmeirion-village.com
www.portmeirion-village.com

Castle Cottage, Harlech

This cottage-style restaurant with rooms has grown with four large boutique suites offering superb comfort. Cooking is mature with solid skill at all levels from homely dishes such as lamb shoulder to contemporary style with local Dyffryn veal and asparagus. Fresh fish from Barmouth include Dover sole, bass, rock prawns, crab and lobster. Servings are generous and the ambience is relaxing and enjoyable.
Y Llech, Harlech LL46 2YL
T: 01766 780479
E: glyn@castlecottageharlech.co.uk
www.castlecottageharlech.co.uk

Castle Hotel, Conwy

This splendid former coaching inn, now refurbished, retains the Shakespearean portraits for the restaurant theme. Cooking is highly competent with modish style. Local Conwy crab, bass, monkfish and mussels, local lamb and Welsh Black beef come with layers of flavours and accompaniments. Finish with gourmet desserts and Welsh farm cheeses. Large comfortable contemporary-styled bedrooms.
High Street, Conwy LL32 8DB
T: 01492 582800
E: mail@castlewales.co.uk
www.castlewales.co.uk

Corn Mill, Llangollen

Superbly positioned overlooking the Dee rapids, with outdoor decking for relaxed eating and drinking.
Dee Lane, Llangollen LL20 7PN
T: 01978 869555

Dylanwad Da, Dolgellau

This long-standing town bistro is renowned for its home-cooked country dishes served in the informality of a true bistro. Pot roasts and slow bakes excel, particularly as the style has kept in tune with contemporary culinary thinking. Treatment of fish and shellfish shows broad understanding of ingredients. The puddings and wine list complete the passion.
2 Ffos-y-Felin, Dolgellau LL40 1BS
T: 01341 422870
E: Dylan@dylanwad.co.uk
www.dylanwad.co.uk

Gales, Llangollen

Characterful wine bar with rooms, hearty food and great wines.
18 Bridge Street, Llangollen LL20 8PF
T: 01978 860089
E: info@galesofllangollen.co.uk
www.galesofllangollen.co.uk

George III, Penmaenpool

The most wonderful location has comfortable bedrooms overlooking the estuary and a very busy bar serving a selection of pub food.
Penmaenpool, Dolgellau LL40 1YD
T: 01341 422525
E: hotel@georgethethird.co.uk
www.georgethethird.co.uk

Granvilles, Criccieth

Café food by day and an evening menu of hearty bistro cooking.
28 High Street, Criccieth LL52 0BT
T: 01766 522506

Groes Inn, near Conwy

Beautifully located above the Conwy Valley this popular hostelry serves generous home-cooked food in an informal ambience.
Tyn-y-Groes, Conwy LL32 8TN
T: 01492 650545
E: reception@groesinn.co.uk
www.groesinn.com

Hand Inn, Llanarmon DC

This is a true local hostelry in this remote drovers' village. Welcoming fires and real ales with a hearty menu of lamb from the Berwyns and Ceiriog Valley trout set the style. Simpler pub food or full restaurant dining are on offer, both presented with skill and care. Comfortable homely accommodation.
Llanarmon DC, Ceiriog Valley, Llangollen LL20 7LD
T: 01691 600666
E: reception@thehandhotel.co.uk
www.thehandhotel.co.uk

Harp Inn, Llandwrog

Bustling bar bistro with hearty home-cooked family food.
Llandwrog, Caernarfon LL54 5SY
T: 01286 831071

Hotel Portmeirion

Wonderfully set on the Glaslyn Estuary the restaurant has the feel of an ocean liner with light modern fabrics. The lavish style of the food matches the eccentric décor of the public rooms. Expect local salt marsh lamb, Welsh Black beef, Anglesey pork, Conwy crab, bass and mussels. It's very popular for weddings and functions. Stylish bedrooms and suites have amazing views.
Portmeirion LL48 6ET
T: 01766 770000
E: hotel@portmeirion-village.com
www.portmeirion-village.com

Kinmel Arms, Abergele

In an elevated greenfield setting this gastro pub with rooms has a colonial feel and is very popular with locals.
The Village, St George, Abergele LL22 9BP
T: 01745 832207
www.thekinmelarms.co.uk

Le Gallois, Penmaenmawr

Honest and confident country cooking of wonderfully fresh local ingredients make this small bistro a most popular venue. There is lamb, beef and duck for carnivores, lobster, crab, mussels and bass for fish lovers. Enjoy the generous puddings, fair prices for food and wines and happy service.
Pantyrafon, Penmaenmawr LL34 6AD
T: 01492 623820

Liverpool Arms, Menai Bridge

Country cooking in a traditional pub.
St. Georges Road, Menai Bridge LL59 5EY
T: 01248 712453

Llety Bodfor, Aberdyfi

Beautiful boutique guesthouse with superb décor and comfort.
Bodfor Terrace, Aberdyfi LL35 0EA
T: 01654 767475
E: bodfor@btopenworld.com
www.lletybodfor.co.uk

Award winning chef Chris Chown at Plas Bodegroes. Its reputation is based upon the modern interpretation of traditional dishes, concentrating on local ingredients.

Lobster Pot, Church Bay
As the name implies fresh seafood is the star in this former tea rooms that served lobster salads in the 1950s. The aquatic menu draws from the lobster ponds next door and trawler-landed fish from the Isle with some sound meat dishes. It's probably the best value menu and wine list in the area.
Church Bay, near Holyhead, Anglesey LL65 4EY
T: 01407 730588

Maes-y-Neuadd, Talsarnau
This mansion in the wooded hills behind Harlech has a dedicated management caring for the luxury rooms, cuisine and grounds. Food is highly skilled from first rate local ingredients cooked with flair and a certain flamboyance. Expect the best lamb from the mountains and seafood from the local boats with vegetables and fruits from their own garden. Dinner has a finale of magnificent desserts.

Talsarnau, near Harlech LL47 6YA
T: 01766 780200 E: maes@neuadd.com
www.neuadd.com

Manorhaus, Ruthin
This contemporary boutique hotel has a cutting edge interior design, with comforts and arts working in harmony. A tasty menu is served in the conservatory restaurant.
10 Well Street, Ruthin LL15 1AH
T: 01824 704830
E: post@manorhaus.com
www.manorhaus.com

Merrion Hotel, Llandudno
Traditional seafront hotel with exceedingly fine home cuisine.
Promenade, Llandudno LL30 2LN
T: 01492 860022
E: enquires@merrion-hotel.co.uk
www.merrion-hotel.co.uk

Moelwyn, Criccieth
Competent Welsh country fare in a comfortable seaside hotel.
Mona Terrace, Criccieth LL52 0HG
T: 01766 522500
E: enquiries@themoelwyn.co.uk
www.themoelwyn.co.uk

Neuadd Lwyd Country House, Llanfair PG
Near the town with the longest name this country house hotel has a high reputation for its modern cooking of Welsh ingredients.
Penmynydd, Llanfairpwllgwyngyll, Anglesey LL61 5BX
T: 01248 715005 E: post@neuaddlwyd.co.uk
www.neuaddlwyd.co.uk

Old Rectory Country House, Llansanffraid Glan Conwy
Truly luxurious bed and breakfast in a beautifully furnished country house.
Llanrwst Road, Llansanffraid Glan Conwy, Conwy LL28 5LF
T: 01492 580611
www.oldrectorycountryhouse.co.uk

● True Taste
Award winners

Paysanne, Deganwy

This ever popular restaurant serves honest home-cooked food in country style dishes from local suppliers.
147 Station Road, Deganwy, Conwy LL31 9EJ
T: 01492 582079
www.paysannedeganwy.co.uk

Pen Y Bwlch, Rhiw, Pwllheli

This delightfully located, small, tasteful guest house serves freshest food from the Llŷn with great commitment to highest quality at reasonable prices.
Rhiw, Pwllheli LL53 8AF
T: 01758 780288
E: info@annesmithglassdesigns.co.uk
www.annesmithglassdesigns.co.uk

Penbrynbach, Aberdaron

Freshest shellfish and seafood from the waters of the Llŷn in a country bistro setting.
Penbryn Bach, Uwch Mynydd, Pwllheli LL53 8BY
T: 01758 760216

Penhelig Arms, Aberdyfi

The Pen combines a true local pub with a modern brasserie restaurant, plus comfortable accommodation, boutique rooms and magnificent contemporary suites. It buzzes with life all year with locals and visitors enjoying the honestly cooked fare of salt marsh lamb, beef, poultry, local bass, crab and lobster and many pub dishes. It has the finest choice of wines at truly rural prices.
Terrace Road, Aberdyfi LL35 0LT
T: 01654 767215 E: info@penheligarms.com
www.penheligarms.com

Penmaenuchaf Hall, Penmaenpool

This magnificent stone mansion in the woods above the Mawddach Estuary has spacious rooms and a calm ambience. The imaginative modern approach to cuisine comes across on the daily changing, well-balanced menus. Careful combinations of ingredients have lightness and life, with techniques bringing out true flavours. Suites and bedrooms have the highest standards of décor and comfort.
Penmaenpool, Dolgellau LL40 1YB
T: 01341 422129 E: relax@penhall.co.uk
www.penhall.co.uk

Plas Bodegroes, Pwllheli ●

For over twenty years this has been a haven of gastronomy and tranquility. Local food featured very strongly before it was even written about. Turbot, brill, bass, scallops, lamb, venison, Welsh Black beef and bacon are all from Llŷn. The creative style has earned a Michelin star for over fifteen years, and many new classic Welsh dishes originated here. This style carries through to the quality of service in the restaurant. Superb grounds, beautiful bedrooms, classic and modern Welsh cuisine complete the scene.
Nefyn Road, Pwllheli LL53 5TH
T: 01758 612363
E: gunna@bodegroes.co.uk
www.bodegroes.co.uk

Plas Tan-yr-Allt, Porthmadog

This hillside hotel has been refurbished to a boutique style, blending traditional features with modern. A communal dining table has good local fare.
High Street, Porthmadog LL49 9PG
T: 01766 513829
E: info@sts-holidays.co.uk
www.snowdoniatourist.com

Porth Tocyn Hotel, Abersoch

The clifftop hotel which overlooks Tremadog Bay to Snowdonia has the longest serving restaurant in The Good Food Guide outside London. The cooking puts very innovative and international touches to prime Welsh ingredients. The ambience created is of a sophisticated dinner party, complete with a help yourself table groaning with desserts and cheese. Cottagey comfortable

Hotel Portmeirion is a stylish hotel with an award winning art deco style dining room, set at the heart of Portmeirion village. (page 27)

bedrooms guarantee a relaxing stay.
Bwlchtocyn, Abersoch LL53 7BU
T: 01758 713303
E: bookings@porthtocyn.fsnet.co.uk
www.porth-tocyn-hotel.co.uk

The Quay Hotel, Deganwy

This magnificent new spa hotel on the old quay at Deganwy has splendid views over the estuary to Conwy Castle and the hills of Penmaenmawr. The elevated restaurant aims at a contemporary brasserie style using the abundance of local food from land and sea. Many of the rooms and suites show its stunning location.
Deganwy Quay, Deganwy, Conwy LL31 9DJ
T: 01492 564100
E: info@quayhotel.com
www.quayhotel.com

Queen's Head, Glanwydden

This is the personification of a local pub and restaurant. The extended dining areas, terrace and kitchen retain the original ambience. The menu covers many fresh ingredients including Conwy mussels, crab, plaice and bass, lamb, beef and game in season. Cooking is competent, presentations are hearty and flavours positive through to delicious desserts.
Glanwydden, Conwy LL31 9JP
T: 01492 546570
E: enquiries@queensheadglanwydden.co.uk
www.queensheadglanwydden.co.uk

Rhiwafallen, Caernarfon

This country farmhouse has the most modern interior design in subtle shades and a conservatory restaurant with a seasonal menu of locally sourced produce.
Llandwrog, Caernarfon LL54 5SW
T: 01286 830172
www.rhiwafallen.co.uk

Rhos Harbour Bistro, Colwyn Bay

Popular modern family bistro in a beautiful harbour location.
Marine Drive, Rhos-on-Sea, Colwyn Bay LL28 4NL
T: 01492 543306
www.rhosharbourbistro.co.uk

Ruby, Menai Bridge

Modern bistro with Welsh and international dishes.
Dale Street, Menai Bridge LL59 5AW
T: 01248 714999
www.rubymenai.co.uk

Seahorse Seafood Bistro, Llandudno

Basement bistro with lots of aquatic specialities in a relaxed ambience.
7 Church Walks, Llandudno LL30 2HD
T: 01492 875315
www.the-seahorse.co.uk

Seiont Manor, Caernarfon

Luxury hotel with country house cooking.
Llanrug, Caernarfon LL55 2AQ
T: 0845 072 7550

Ship Hotel, Aberdaron

Lobsters, crab and many line caught fish come from the local fishing boats that moor in the lee of the bay. In season this pub-restaurant can be hectic. People queue for lobster that comes in a variety of ways, or a large bowl of mussels, grilled bass, crab salad or meat dishes. It's all served in generous portions and well worth the wait.
Aberdaron, Pwllheli LL53 8BE
T: 01758 760204
E: alunharrison@btconnect.com
www.theshiphotelaberdaron.co.uk

The Ship Inn, Red Wharf Bay

This pub for all seasons is cosy in winter with spacious *al fresco* dining in summer. The high tide laps the terrace, so expect excellent seafood from Ynys Môn, particularly bass, sewin, mussels and crab. The local beef is notable alongside lamb and poultry. Cooking ranges from plain to exotic so suits wide tastes. It's good value including wines and real ale.
Red Wharf Bay, Anglesey LL75 8RJ
T: 01248 852568
E: info@shipinnredwharfbay.co.uk
www.shipinnredwharfbay.co.uk

Soughton Hall and The Stables Bar Restaurant, Northop

This modern brasserie is in the original stables of this grand hotel, a former Bishop's palace.
Northop, Flintshire CH7 6AB
T: 01352 840577
www.soughtonhall.co.uk

St Tudno, Llandudno

This jewel on the sea front has beautifully appointed lounges and the secluded Terrace Restaurant. The cooking from immaculately fresh seafood, local meat and game is highly innovative and to the moment. Intelligent techniques and use of ingredients in subtle and adventurous combinations can be very exciting through to the colourful desserts. Individually designed bedrooms are to exacting standards.
North Promenade, Llandudno LL30 2LP
T: 01492 874411
E: sttudnohotel@btinternet.com
www.st-tudno.co.uk

Sychnant Pass House, Conwy

This beautifully appointed country house in the hills above Conwy has a warmth of hospitality that extends from the comforts to the cuisine.
Sychnant Pass Road, Conwy LL32 8BJ
T: 01492 596868
E: bre@sychnant-pass-house.com
www.sychnant-pass-house.co.uk

Tan-y-Foel, Betws-y-Coed

This remote converted farmhouse overlooks the Conwy Valley. Inside it has the air and tranquillity of the finest boutique hotel with sophisticated in vogue minimalist décor and clever use of fabrics. Truly owner-run in every aspect the one woman kitchen produces brilliant dishes with amazingly skilled judgement. Locally sourced seafood, meat and game shine. Wine recommendations complete the dining experience. Sumptuous bedrooms have every modern comfort.
Capel Garmon, near Betws-y-Coed LL26 0RE
T: 01690 710507 E: enquiries@tyfhotel.co.uk
www.tyfhotel.co.uk

Tir a Mor, Criccieth

This small bistro has a young team cooking generous dishes from local produce.
1 – 3 Mona Terrace, Criccieth LL52 0HG
T: 01766 523084

Trearddur Bay Hotel

This is the home of the Anglesey Oyster and Welsh Produce Festival, held each October. Large hotel with spacious dining room in a beautiful beachside setting.
Lon Isallt, Trearddur, Holyhead, Anglesey LL65 2UN
T: 01407 860301
E: enquires@trearddurbayhotel.co.uk

Hands-on chef Bryan Webb at Tyddyn Llan, Llandrillo.

True Taste Award winners

Tre-Ysgawen Hall Hotel, Llangefni

This imposing Victorian mansion has superb rooms, a large spa with an informal wine bar as well as hotel restaurant.
Capel Coch, Llangefni Anglesey LL77 7UR
T: 01248 750750
E: enquiries@treysgawen-hall.co.uk
www.treysgawen-hall.co.uk

Ty Gwyn Hotel, Betws-y-Coed

This cosy traditional inn serves hearty rural food generously in the bar and dining room.
Betws-y-Coed, Conwy LL24 0SG
T: 01690 710383
www.tygwynhotel.co.uk

Tŷ Newydd, Aberdaron

Fresh seafood from the local boats is the speciality here in the restaurant.
Aberdaron, Pwllheli LL53 8BE
T: 01758 760207
www.gwesty-tynewydd.co.uk

Ty'n Rhos, Llanddeiniolen

This spacious farm guest house in verdant grounds has real talent in the kitchen committed to using fresh produce.
These include vegetables and herbs from their garden, fish from the Llŷn and Menai, meat from Anglesey and Snowdonia presented in very creative dishes.
Seion, Llanddeiniolen, near Caernarfon LL55 3AE
T: 01248 670489 E: enquiries@tynrhos.co.uk
www.tynrhos.co.uk

Tyddyn Llan, Llandrillo ●

Innovation and tradition backed up with soundest culinary skills add up to some of the finest cooking in Britain. Everything used in its time with spring lamb, asparagus, lobster, and sewin leading onto grouse, partridge, pheasant and venison as the seasons unfold. Presentations are lighter in summer, rich and darker in winter. Total accuracy applies equally to seared scallops as it does to Sunday roast beef.
Llandrillo, near Corwen LL21 0ST
T: 01490 440264
E: tyddynllan@compuserve.com
www.tyddynllan.co.uk

Waterfront, Trearddur Bay

This spectacularly located beachfront pub-with-food offers meals made largely with local ingredients.
Lon Isallt, Trearddur Bay, Holyhead LL65 2UT
T: 01407 860006

West Arms, Llanarmon DC

This seventeenth century hostelry has oak beams, log fires, inglenooks and cosy bedrooms and a mouthwatering menu. Pheasant come from the Ceiriog Valley, lamb from the Berwyns, there's local Welsh Black beef and seafood from the North Wales coast.
Llanarmon DC, near Llangollen LL20 7LD
T: 01691 600665
E: gowestarms@aol.com
www.thewestarms.co.uk

The White Eagle Inn, Holyhead

A refurbished pub close to the sea serves wonderfully fresh seafood.
Rhoscolyn, Anglesey
T: 01407 860267
E: white.eagle@timpson.com
www.white-eagle.co.uk

White Horse Inn, Denbigh

Very popular traditional inn and restaurant.
Llandyrnog, Denbigh LL16 4HG
T: 01824 790582

Y Gegin Fawr, Aberdaron

Once a communal kitchen where medieval pilgrims took sustenance on their way to Bardsey Island, this café offers homemade cakes and scones, local crab and lobster, and other delights – to eat in or to take away for a picnic.
Aberdaron, Llŷn LL53 8BE
T: 01758 760359

Y Meirionnydd

What was once Dolgellau's old jail has now been refurbished into a cosy restaurant. Meals are straightforward, using local ingredients such as ice creams and sorbets from Pembrokeshire, Ceredigion Bay Sea Bass and cheeses such as Gorwedd Caerffili and Red Llangloffen. Service is efficient but unobtrusive.
Smithfield Square, Dolgellau LL 40 1ES
T: 01341 422554
E: info@themeirionnydd.com
www.themeirionnydd.com

Ye Olde Bulls Head, Beaumaris

Eat in either the modern brasserie or stylish Loft Restaurant where modern cuisine shines. Ingredients are sourced locally, including St George's mushrooms and cèpes from Great Orme's Head, crab from Holyhead, oysters and mussels from Brynsiencyn. Intelligent food pairings and combinations demonstrate the sound cooking and adaptable skill backed up by a great wine list.
Castle Street, Beaumaris LL58 8AP
T: 01248 810329
E: info@bullsheadinn.co.uk
www.bullsheadinn.co.uk

Yr Hen Fecws, Porthmadog

Homely cooking in a comfortable, small restaurant with rooms.
16 Lombard Street, Porthmadog LL49 9AP
T: 01766 514625
E: enquiries@henfecws.com
www.henfecws.com

Contemporary fashionable décor at Ye Olde Bulls Head, Beaumaris, blends skilfully with the traditional style of the sixteenth century inn.

North Wales: where to buy and producers

Farm shops throughout North Wales such as Abbey Grange Farm Shop and Bellis Brothers produce and sell an array of seasonal vegetables.

Welsh Black fillet steak from Edwards of Conwy makes a hearty meal.

Owen Roberts & Son is a family butcher in Amwlch specialising in lamb and homemade produce.

A host of producers

North Wales has to be one of the greenest parts of Britain with a wonderfully diverse terrain and coastline. Hence the range of produce available is immense. In almost every small town or village there are some shops selling local produce. Farm shops and farmers' markets give even more choice. But it is not as shopping in a one stop multiple. Visit a few of these places and there are plenty of local characters to encounter.

Food festivals

There are major food festivals in North Wales held at Llangollen, Pwllheli, and Conwy. Each has a large number of food stalls from all across North Wales selling a big range of food. There will be fresh organic meat, cooked, cured and smoked meats, vegetables, dairy produce including artisan cheeses, ice cream and yogurt, bread and cakes, confectionery, chutneys and preserves, drinks including liqueurs, country wines, artisan beer and cider. The Conwy and Llŷn festivals both also have a good range of fresh fish from local landings, weather permitting, plus shellfish, smoked and cured fish and prepared seafoods.

Each of the festivals stage cooking demonstrations where it's possible to learn some tips on how to cook the produce from the leading chefs of the region and some celebrities.

Good food of the region that will certainly feature at these festivals includes: Gorau Glas cheese; Village Dairy Yogurts; smoked meat and fish from Derimôn Smokery; organic meat from the Rhug Estate; Elwy Valley lamb; handmade pies from Harvies of Nercwys; pâtés from Patchwork Traditional Foods; artisan and spelt bread from Dai Chef's Bread of Heaven; seafood specialities from Pysgod Llŷn and Llŷn Fishermen's Co-operative; traditional ales from Conwy Brewery, Bragdy Ynys Môn and Great Orme Brewery; Ralph's Farmhouse Cider and many others.

The glorious oyster

The Anglesey Oyster Festival, held appropriately in September, is quite different. It promotes seafood, particularly oysters in numerous restaurants and pubs throughout the isle. There are lots of promotional menus featuring local seafood and beers and fun activities throughout the week, all aimed to seduce people into enjoying the wonderful oyster.

Farmers' markets bring the customer and producer together. Regular markets are mostly held monthly at Wrexham, Colwyn Bay, Ruthin, Rhug Estate and Bangor. There is a weekly vegetable and other local produce market held at Ruthin in the old market hall. Llangefni open market is held every Thursday and Saturday. Wrexham has its permanent indoor market in Chester Street open normal daily shop hours.

Farm shops

Farm shops have become increasingly popular, and many in North Wales present quite a broad offering of their own produce and that of others from the region and further afield. Abbey Grange Farm Shop, just outside Llangollen, has a range of seasonal vegetables and their own pork. Bellis Brothers at Holt, near Wrexham, grow their own fruit and vegetables and also sell local meat and dairy produce. In summer pick-your-own fruit is popular and a family run restaurant serves good home-cooked food. Plas Farm, Anglesey, and Lewis's farm shop, Wrexham, also stock fine produce.

Rhug Estate farm shop near Corwen sells organic meat exclusively produced on the estate. Pedigree Aberdeen Angus beef is hung for 28 days in the state-of-the-art cold rooms on the estate before being butchered. Welsh lamb comes from the Corwen Estate and also salt marsh lamb from their farm on the Llŷn Peninsula. Part of this farm is low lying and floods at spring tides, producing summer salt marsh pasture for grazing lambs over the summer and autumn. Pork comes from their estate in Shropshire where the pigs forage the fields after the organic vegetables have been harvested, producing a wonderful flavour to the meat. Free-range organic chicken roam the fields close to the farm shop. The slow-growing French *belle rouge* variety produces close-textured meat of incomparable quality. The butchers make their own sausages, burgers and meat pies. Bacon and ham is dry-cured on the estate. The farm shop sells a range of Welsh and other organic produce. The burger bar serves their organic burgers, bacon sandwiches and various meats in rolls. Plans are well advanced to build a new farm shop and restaurant.

Home grown

Glasfryn Farm Shop near Pwllheli sells meat from their own farm including Welsh Black beef, Welsh lamb, Cig Moch Penllŷn bacon plus a selection of Welsh farmhouse cheeses, vegetables, homemade jams, sauces and confectionery.

On Anglesey, on the A4080 towards Brynsiencyn, Hooton's Home Grown in Gwydryn Hir sells exclusively vegetables and fruit from their own farm. Everything is seasonal and only available then. Root vegetables, potatoes, leeks, cauliflower, asparagus, courgettes, tomatoes and salads, plus strawberries, blackcurrants, raspberries, gooseberries are all available in season. They rear fine quality free-range pigs and poultry to sell in the shop, also making their own sausages and bacon, plus a large range of meat pies. They make chutneys and preserves from their own fruit and vegetables and bake a range of cakes and puddings.

Independent butchers

There are many independent butchers who have weathered the competition from the multiples and are now reaping the benefit. Those who have specialised in quality meat, particularly such as salt marsh and mountain lamb, Welsh beef and free-range pork and chicken now have a growing customer base. Independent butchers pride themselves on the proper maturation of meat. Hanging beef for several weeks vastly improves its quality, flavour and tenderness, and lamb needs a similar yet shorter treatment. Many produce excellent by-products such as sausages, burgers, faggots, cooked meats, and cure their own bacon and ham.

It is worth talking to them about their produce, its origin and maturation. Of particular note, Edwards of Conwy always stands out as the shining example of what an independent butcher can achieve. Their shop in an old bank in the High Street has a most impressive display of beautifully butchered meat. They know the origin of everything and certificates adorn the walls. Their range of homemade pies is impressive. Their sausages are now so famous that they have a separate business in Morfa Conwy called the Traditional Welsh Sausage Company that supplies throughout the country and to some multiples.

T J Roberts in Bala is a traditional butcher specialising in meat from the local area and hence sells fine pasture lamb and beef, free-range pork and poultry, plus home-cooked pies, faggots and sausages. Top quality Welsh beef is expertly butchered at John Swain Williams of Menai Bridge. All their meat is from farms on Anglesey and also includes pasture lamb, pork and free-range poultry.

Cigydd Aberdyfi have their own farm and source all meat within 10 miles of this resort town. Mountain lamb comes from the lofty heights of Cadair Idris, the hills surrounding the town itself, and the salt marshes of the Dyfi Estuary. Beef, pork and poultry are all from local farms they have known for generations. Another notable butcher in Amlwch is Owen Roberts.

Several of the Spar shops have impressive butcher's counters. Of particular note is the entrepreneurial Spar in Pwllheli that has an informal purchasing group with the local farms. The quality of the meat is first rate and the prices competitive as they deal directly with farms. Their range of Welsh cheeses and all other locally sourced produce is highly impressive. On a more modest scale but highly commendable is Baldwyn's Spar in Towyn with a fine butcher's counter plus farmhouse cheeses, dairy and general produce.

Delicatessens

Specialist shops and delicatessens have an increasing range of Welsh produce reflecting the increasing availability of local and specialist foods. Blas Ar Fwyd

in Llanrwst has been a leader with an impressive set up that includes a bakery, delicatessen, wine shop and Amser Da restaurant. They have the widest range of farmhouse cheeses, smoked and cured fish and meat from producers such as Cig Moch Penllŷn, Llandudno Smokery and Derimôn. Their wholesale division supplies many others across North Wales. An outside catering division can cope with functions of any size.

Several new delicatessens have opened in the area. Of note Sarah's Deli in Beaumaris, the Saffron delicatessen in Llanberis and Iechyd Da in Betws-y-Coed show the interest in high quality specialist food.

Seafood

In the past fresh seafood has ironically been the most difficult to find in an area with such a long coastline that has numerous fishing boats working the inshore waters. The bulk of the landings go directly to the

Blas Farm pride themselves on selling finest quality local and Welsh produce including traditional homemade meals using the finest ingredients.

Edwards of Conwy has won several awards for for its innovation and excellence in meat products, particularly for their sausages.

Crab is landed regularly from fishermen in North Wales.

Classic moules marinière – shallots, butter, white wine, herbs – that's all – basic, rustic and utterly delicious.

lucrative Continental markets disappearing live in large vivier lorries.

The Llŷn Fishermen's Co-operative is based at Pwllheli and co-ordinates the landings of boats around the coast. Pwllheli Seafoods utilises as much of the fresh fish as possible to supply hotels restaurants and retailers throughout North Wales, supplemented by fish landed in other ports. Their retail shop has a regular selection of bass, mullet, sole, plaice and skate, plus mussels, crab and lobster from the area. In season they carry a large selection of game from estates in North Wales. The close-by Pysgod Llŷn Seafoods has developed seafood processing and makes a range of seafood sauces, soup, pies, terrines and ready meals.

A number of fishing families have always done crab processing on a domestic or cottage industry scale, selling dressed crab from their house or to local pubs and restaurants. Selective Seafoods is in a remote location between Nefyn and Aberdaron. They purchase crab and lobster plus bass and prime fish from the boats at the tiny sheltered mooring at Porth Colmon. Follow signs in the hedges to their small processing plant where they sell to the public and dispatch to restaurants.

Mussels

The Conwy Mussel Company on the quay has purification tanks and will sell by the kilo to the public. They are the main suppliers to the catering trade in North Wales and beyond. Oysters from Wales's only oyster farm, together with mussels, can be bought from Menai Oysters at their purification plant near Brynsiencyn on Anglesey, or purchased by mail order anywhere in Britain.

Smokeries

The largest fish dealer is The Fish Shop and Llandudno Smokery in Builder Street, Llandudno. They have a large retail shop plus wholesale distribution to shops and restaurants. They have developed the smokery into a major business and now produce smoked salmon, trout, bass, mackerel, cod, haddock plus a range of meat and game. Jo Lewis in Porthmadog and Gill's Plaice fish shop in Aberdyfi are both notable fishmongers in their area.

Fresh farmed trout plus cured and smoked trout can be bought directly from Chirk Trout Farm and Smokery. At Old Forge Trout Farm, Bodfari, you can fish for your supper then pay for it and take it home to cook as fresh as possible. Other similar trout farms are at Marian Mill, Trelawnyd, Rhyl and Forrest Hill, Whitford, Holywell.

fine mussels come from Port Penrhyn, Brynsiencyn and the Conwy Estuary

● True Taste
Award winners

The True Taste / Gwir Flas Food and Drink Awards

The True Taste / Gwir Flas Food and Drink Awards, are part of the commitment by the Welsh Assembly Government, Food and Market Development Division, to develop and build the Welsh food sector and awareness of the Welsh food brand 'Wales the True Taste'. The True Taste Awards recognise quality, innovation and excellence in the Welsh food and drink industry with more than 500 products and services judged each year. Winners can use the award on their products for three years. Award winners listed here are from 2005, 2006 and 2007.

markets, shops, specialists and producers in North Wales

Abbey Grange Farm Shop
Sell a range of veg in season and produce their own Welsh pork, bread jams and chutneys.
Llangollen LL20 8DD
T: 01978 869321

Anglesey Hampers
Food from the area – cheese, seafood, smoked products, drinks.
Fferm Ty Buarth, Dothan,
Ty Croes, Anglesey LL63 5YA
T: 01407 720231
www.angleseyhampers.co.uk

Ash Manor Cheese
Large farm producer of cheddar cheese.
63 Clywedog Road North, Wrexham
Industrial Estate, Wrexham LL13 9XN
T: 01978 660112
E: ashmanorcheese@breath.co.uk
www.ashmanor.com

Baldwyn's (Spar)
General stores with Welsh produce.
16 High Street, Tywyn LL36 9AD
T: 01654 710452

Beef Direct
Anglesey beef from the shop and mail order.
Plas Coedana, Llannerch-y-medd,
Anglesey LL71 8AA
T: 01247 470387 E: info@beefdirect.net
www.beefdirect.net

Bellis Brothers Farm Shop
Fruit and vegetables, farm shop and PYO.
Wrexham Road, Holt, Wrexham LL13 9YU
T: 01829 270304

Blas Ar Fwyd ●
Top Welsh delicatessen, bakery, restaurant and outside catering.
25 Heol Yr Orsaf, Llanrwst LL26 0BT
T: 01492 640215
E: info@blasarfwyd.com
www.blasarfwyd.com

Blue Water Flatfish Farm
Turbot, halibut and bass are farmed in large tanks at a disused quarry.
Dinmor Quarry, Penmon, Anglesey LL58 8SN
T: 01248 490894

Bragdy Ynys Môn
Small brewery with distinctive ales.
Cae Cwta Mawr, Talwrn, Llangefni LL77 7SD
T: 01248 723801
E: martyn@angleseyale.co.uk

Bron y Gan Lamb
Specialist prepared lamb dishes and fresh meat.
Bron y Gan, Llanegryn, Tywyn LL36 9UF
T: 01654 711553

Brooklyn Farm
Organic meat, vegetables, dry goods and dairy.
Sealand Road, Deeside CH5 2LQ
T: 01244 881209

Bwydlyn
Beef, cured meats, mutton, bresaola, lamb.
11 Bank Place, Porthmadog LL49 9AA
T: 01766 512288
E: info@bwydlyn.co.uk
www.bwydlyn.co.uk

Cadwalader's Ice Cream
Real dairy ice cream.
Parc Amaeth, Llanystumdwy, Criccieth
LL20 0LJ
T: 01766 522478
E: info@cadwaladersicecream.co.uk
www.cadwaladersicecream.co.uk

Calon Lan Food Olew Camelina ●
Oils refined naturally from less usual
vegetables and grains.
Llys Goferydd, Bryn Cefni, Llangefni,
Anglesey LL77 7XA
T: 01758 612621
E: post@calonlanfood.com
www.calonlanfood.com

Cegin Famau
Home-cooked dishes to original and
traditional Welsh recipes.
Unit 7A Colomendy Industrial Estate,
Denbigh LL16 5TA
T: 01745 818811

Chirk Trout Farm
Farmed trout, fresh and smoked.
Chirk LL14 5BL
T: 01691 773101
E: shop@chirktroutfarm.com
www.chirktroutfarm.com

Cig Moch Penllŷn
Dry-cured bacon and hams.
Glasfryn Parc, Y Ffôr, Pwllheli LL53 6RD
T: 01766 810044 E: info@cigmoch.co.uk
www.cigmoch.co.uk

Cig Môn Cymru
Quality lamb and beef from Anglesey.
Trading Estate, Llangefni LL77 7JA
T: 01248 750212
E: cigmon@hotmail.com
www.cigmon.co.uk

Cigydd Aberdyfi ●
Specialists in salt marsh and mountain
lamb and farm beef.
3 Copperhill Street, Aberdyfi LL35 0EU
T: 01654 767223
E: smfowles@yahoo.co.uk

Conwy Brewery
Small brewery with distinctive range of light
and dark ales.
Unit 3, Parc Caer Seion, Conwy LL32 8FA
T: 01492 585287
E: enquires@conwybrewery.co.uk
www.conwybrewery.co.uk

Conwy Mussels Co
Purified mussels on the quay directly
from fishery.
The Mussel Centre, The Quay, Conwy
LL32 8BB
T: 01492 592689

Conwy Valley Meats
Prime farm quality lamb and beef.
Parry Road, Llanrwst LL26 0DG
T: 01492 641861
E: conwyvalleymeats@btconnect.com

Dai Chef, Bread of Heaven, Chirk
Original recipe spelt and artisan breads.
2 Crogen, Lodgevale Park, Chirk LL14 5BN
T: 01691 773241 E: daichef@aol.com

Decantae Mineral Water
Quality presentation of fine mineral water.
Tir Llwyd Industrial Estate, Kinmel Bay
LL18 5JA
T: 01745 343504
E: sales@decantae.co.uk
www.decantae.co.uk

● True Taste
Award winners

Derimôn Smokery ●

Produces a wide range of hot and cold
smoked specialities including salmon, cod,
haddock and kippers, Anglesey oak-smoked
sea salt, smoked cheese and butter.
Deri Isaf, Dulas Bay, Anglesey LL70 9DX
T: 01248 410536
E: derimon_smokery@btconnect.com
www.derimonsmokery.co.uk

Direct Welsh Lamb

Local lamb sold through shop and internet.
Esgair Farm, Aberdyfi LL35 0SP
T: 01654 767101
www.welshlambdirect.co.uk

Edwards of Conwy ●

Finest quality butcher, home produced
sausages, cured and baked products.
18 High Street, Conwy LL32 8DE
T: 01492 592443
E: sales@edwardsofconwy.co.uk
www.edwardsofconwy.co.uk

Elwy Valley Lamb

Marketing group for high quality lamb from
nominated farms.
Rose Hill Cottage, Henllan LL16 5BA
T: 01745 813552
E: tilly@elwyvalleylamb.co.uk
www.elwyvalleylamb.co.uk

Gill's Plaice

Fresh and prepared seafood.
16 Chapel Square, Aberdyfi LL35 0EL
T: 01654 767875

Glasfryn Farm Shop ●

Farm shop on leisure park; estate lamb,
beef, Llŷn pork and bacon.
Y Ffôr Pwllheli LL53 6RD
T: 01766 810044
E: farmshop@glasfryn.co.uk
www.siop-glasfryn.com

Gorau Glas Cheese

Artisan soft blue cheese.
Quirt Farm, Dwyran, Anglesey LL61 6BZ
T: 01248 430570

Great Orme Brewery

A growing reputation for producing quality
real ale served in pubs, restaurants and
hotels in North Wales.
Nant-y-Cywarch Farm, Glan Conwy, Colwyn
Bay LL28 5PP
T: 01492 580 548
E: info@greatormebrewery.co.uk
www.greatormebrewery.co.uk

Halen Môn/The Anglesey Sea Salt Company ●

Organic sea salt from local waters.
Brynsiencyn, Anglesey LL61 6TQ
T: 01248 430871 E: enq@seasalt.co.uk
www.seasalt.co.uk

Halo Foods

Healthy snacks from natural grains.
Tywyn LL36 9LW
T: 01654 711171 E: sales@halofoods.co.uk
www.halofoods.co.uk

Harvie's

Highest quality homemade traditional pies
and preserves.
Waen Farm, Nercwys, Mold CH7 4EW
T: 01352 751285
E: pastry5@btinternet.com

Hooton's Farm Shop

Home grown and reared vegetables, fruits,
pork and poultry, PYO.
Gwydryn Hir, Brynsiencyn LL61 6HQ
T: 01248 430344
E: Info@hootonshomegrown.com
www.hootonshomegrown.com

Iechyd Da Delicatessen

Modern delicatessen Welsh cheeses and
general foods.
Station Road, Betws-y-Coed LL24 0AG
T: 01690 710944
www.delinorthwales.co.uk

Joe Lewis

Fresh fish, fruit and vegetables.
98 High Street, Porthmadog LL49 9NW
T: 01766 512229

John Jones & Son
Traditional butcher, fresh fish, vegetables and fruit.
29 Clwyd Street, Ruthin LL15 1HH
T: 01824 702737
E: info@johnjonesandson.com
www.johnjonesandson.com

KK Finefoods ●
Large manufacturer for food service industry.
Estuary House, Deeside Industrial Estate, Deeside CH5 2UA
T: 01244 286200
E: info@kkfinefoods.com
www.kkfinefoods.com

Lewis Farm Shop
Seasonal own grown vegetables and fruit.
Brook Cottage, Eyton, Wrexham LL13 0SW
T: 01978 780852

Llandudno Smokery & Fish Shop
Smoked fish and fresh seafood specialists.
Unit 4, The Old Abattoir, Builder Street Llandudno LL30 1DR
T: 01492 870430
E: info@llandudnosmokery.co.uk
www.thesmokery.co.uk

Llechwedd Meats (Anglesey Choice)
Quality meat from Anglesey.
Unit 4 –6 Gaerwen Industrial Estate, Gaerwen, Anglesey LL60 6HR
T: 01248 422073

Llŷn Aquaculture
Consultants in fish farming.
Afonwen Farm, Chwilog, Pwllheli LL53 6TX
T: 01766 810904

Llŷn Fishermen's Co
Daily landings of fresh fish around Llŷn Peninsula.
Blaen-y-Ddol, Edern, Pwllheli LL53 6JA
T: 01758 720656

Megans Kitchen
Home baked specialities.
The Bishop Trevor, Llangollen LL20 8SN
T: 01978 861453

Menai Oysters
Oysters and mussels from Menai Straits.
Tal-y-Bont Bach, Llanfairpwll, Anglesey LL61 6UU
T: 01248 430878

Myti Mussels
Farmed mussels for large scale export.
Port Penrhyn, Bangor LL57 4HN
T: 01248 354878

Owen Roberts a'i Fab
Anglesey meat specialising in lamb and homemade produce.
Corwas, Amlwch LL68 9ET
T: 01407 830277

Old Forge Trout Farm
Trout rearing for sport and eating.
Mold Road, Bodfari LL16 4DW
T: 01745 710305
www.oldforgetroutfarm.com

Organic Aran Lamb ●
Quality lamb from natural pasture.
Cwmonnen Farm, Llanuwchllyn, Bala LL23 7UG
T: 01678 540603 E: sales@aran-lamb.co.uk
www.aran-lamb.co.uk

Organic Stores
Comprehensive selection of local fresh food.
7 Mwrog Street, Ruthin LL15 1LB
T: 01824 705796

Party Cooks
Caterers for private and corporate events.
38 Cardiff Road, Pwllheli LL53 3NR
T: 01758 612140
www.partycookspwllheli.co.uk

Patchwork Traditional Food Company

Pâté specialists, quality pies and meals.
Llys Parcwr, Ruthin LL15 1NJ
T: 01824 705832
E: sales@patchwork-pate.co.uk
www.patchwork-pate.co.uk

Plas Farm Denbigh Farmhouse Dairy Ice Cream ●

Ice cream from own herd's milk.
Celtic House, Gaerwen, Anglesey LL60 6HR
T: 01248 422011
E: sales@plas-farm.co.uk
www.plas-farm.co.uk

Plas Llanfair Organics

Preserves and chutneys.
Plas Llanfair, Tyn-y-Gongl,
Anglesey LL74 8NU
T: 01248 852316

Plassey Brewery

Cask conditioned ales from small brewery.
The Plassey, Eyton, Wrexham LL13 0SP
T: 01978 781111
www.plasseybrewery.co.uk

Popty'r Bryn

Home baked bara brith, shortbread and toffee.
Cefn Arthen, Brynsiencyn, Anglesey
LL61 6SZ
T: 01248 430223
E: nerys@poptyrbryn.co.uk

Popty'r Dref

Traditional bakery and shop.
Upper Smithfield Street, Dolgellau LL40 1ET
T: 01341 422507

Pwllheli Seafoods

Fresh fish and shellfish for retail and
catering.
Unit 4, Glan Y Don Industrial Estate,
Pwllheli LL53 5YT
T: 01758 614615
E: sales@seafoodandgame.com
www.seafoodandgame.com

Pysgod Llŷn Seafood ●

Fresh seafoods and homemade
seafood dishes.
Y Maes, Pwllheli LL53 5HA
T: 01758 614292
E: sales@llynseafoods.co.uk
www.llynseafoods.co.uk

Rhug Organic Estate ●

Large organic estate rearing lamb, beef,
pork and poultry under Soil Association
standards. Farm shop and café.
Rhug Estate Office, Corwen LL21 0EH
T: 01490 413000 E: contact@rhug.co.uk
www.rhugorganic.com

Roberts of Port Dinorwic

Cooked meats and dishes for food service
industry.
Griffiths Crossing Industrial Estate,
Caernarfon LL55 1TS
T: 01286 676111
E: info@roberts-wales.co.uk
www.roberts-wales.co.uk

Saffron Delicatessen

New style quality delicatessen.
48 High Street, Llanberis LL55 4EU
T: 01286 871777
E: llanberisorganics@tiscali.co.uk
www.llanberisorganics.co.uk

Sarah's Deli

Modern delicatessen.
11 Church Street, Beaumaris LL58 8AB
T: 01248 811534

Selective Seafoods

Fresh crab, lobster and fish from local
boats, and dressed crab specialists.
Ffridd Wen, Tudweiliog, Pwllheli LL53 8BJ
T: 01758 770397
E: mary@selectiveseafoods.com
www.selectiveseafoods.com

Seren Foods

Wine and fruit jellies for meat.
Cae Glas, Glyn Ceiriog, Llangollen LL20 7AB
www.seren-foods.co.uk

Siop Newydd

A wide range of local Welsh products, British and continental specialities displayed on original nineteenth century shelving.
High Street, Criccieth LL52 0EY
T: 01766 522737

Snowdonia Cheese Company

Welsh Cheddar in many novel flavours.
Unit B6, Trem Y Dyffryn, Colomendy Industrial Estate, Denbigh LL16 5TX
T: 01745 813388
E: sales@snowdonia-cheese.co.uk
www.snowdonia-cheese.co.uk

South Caernarfon Creameries

Large co-operative producing high-quality cheese, butter, cream and milk.
Rhydygwystl, Chwilog, Pwllheli LL53 6SB
T: 01766 810251
E: sales@sccwales.co.uk
www.sccwales.co.uk

Spar, Pwllheli

Local supermarket specialising in quality produce and meat from the Llŷn Peninsula.
Y Maes, Pwllheli LL53 5HA
T: 01758 612993
E: info@sparymaes.co.uk

Swain Williams

High quality butcher for Anglesey meat.
2 Bridge Street, Menai Bridge LL59 5DW
T: 01248 712915

T J Roberts & Sons

Traditional butcher with top quality local meat.
Tryweryn House, Bala LL23 7NG
T: 01678 520471

Tipyn Bach Chocolate Company

Luxury chocolates.
Unit G5, Bodnant Gardens, Tal-y-Cafn, Conwy LL28 3RE
T: 01492 650046
E: info@tipynbach.co.uk
www.tipynbach.co.uk

Traditional Welsh Sausage Co

Expert manufacturers of top quality sausages.
Unit 1, Crwst Business Park, Conwy LL32 8HH
T: 01492 576800
E: info@welshsausages.co.uk
www.welshsausages.co.uk

Village Dairy – Llaeth y Llan

Yogurt from local supplies.
Tal-y-Bryn Farm, Llannefydd LL16 5DR
T: 01745 540256
E: llaeth@villagedairy.co.uk
www.villagedairy.co.uk

Welsh Black Cattle Society

Protection and promotion of the native breed.
13 Bangor Street, Caernarfon LL55 1AP
T: 01286 672391
E: welshblack@btclick.com
www.welshblackcattlesociety.org

Welsh Lady Preserves

Traditional preserves, chutneys, jams.
Bron Y Ffôr, Pwllheli LL53 6RL
T: 01766 810496
E: info@welshladypreserves.com
www.welshladypreserves.com

Wenallt Stores

Village stores with many local foods.
Llanbedr LL45 2LD
T: 01341 241220

Worthenbury Wines

The only vineyard in North Wales, producing quality red and white wine from classic grape varieties.
The Old Rectory, Worthenbury, Wrexham LL13 0AW
T: 01948 770257
E: sales@worthenburywines.co.uk
www.worthenburywines.co.uk

Wrexham Market

Interesting shopping in the butcher's market for meat, fish and vegetables.
Henblas Street, Wrexham LL13 8AD
T: 01978 29705

Mid Wales

Mid Wales is a land of green, leafy forests, vast hills, lakes, reservoirs and rivers – this is Lake Vyrnwy, with its Victorian Gothic water tower.

Mid Wales

The heartland of Wales, from the Berwyns to the Brecon Beacons, has an abundance of organic land, set amid undulating mountains, forests, hills and river valleys. The meandering Severn, the sylvan Wye, the sewin-leaping Teifi and the trout-filled Usk pass through. The region is dotted with spa towns and drovers' hamlets; former fishing villages are now boutique resorts. Culinary highlights include Radnorshire lamb, organic dairy produce and the seafood of Cardigan Bay.

Welshpool

Machynlleth

Montgomery

Newtown

Aberystwyth

Knighton

Rhayader

Presteigne

Aberaeron

Llandrindod Wells

New Quay

Lampeter

Buith Wells

Cardigan   Llandysul

Llanwrtyd Wells

Hay-on-Wye

Brecon

Crickhowell

Mid Wales: about the area

Indigenous deciduous trees on natural uplands of Mid Wales.

Area

This area includes the counties of Powys and Ceredigion, south of the Berwyn Mountains and the Dyfi Valley, taking in the borderland with England from Chirk in the north to the Black Mountains south of Hay-on-Wye almost to Abergavenny.

It extends across the Brecon Beacons into the upper Swansea Valley and north to the Cambrian Mountains and west to the coast of Cardigan Bay from the Dyfi to the Teifi estuaries.

Rivers

Much of the area is around 400 metres above sea level dissected by a network of rivers. The Severn, Wye and Teifi all originate in Pumlumon, draining this vast upland area with numerous tributaries. The Teifi catchment runs into Cardigan Bay whereas both the Wye and Severn meander their way east eventually flowing into the Bristol Channel. The River Usk drains the south of the area from the Brecon Beacons and Mynydd Epynt.

This area has one of the lowest densities of population in Britain. The economy largely depends on livestock farming and dairy farming particularly in the Teifi Valley. Most of the small towns such as Rhayader, Llangurig, Tregaron and Llandysul were dependent on their livestock markets. Numerous small villages such as Elan, Beulah, Howey, Pumpsaint, and Llansawel were situated on old drovers' trails. The Teifi Valley was the centre of the Welsh woollen industry that sadly declined after the Second World War; now the few mills that remain are capitalising on the designer market for house wares.

Towns

In the Victorian era the custom of taking medicinal spring waters led to the growth of many spa towns. Mid Wales with its clean air and plentiful rainfall has many springs that were developed for this market. The spa towns of Llandrindod Wells, Builth

Fly fishing the tail of the famous salmon pool 'Heirog' on Gromaine, the Upper Wye, near Llyswen where I have caught many fine salmon and trout. 'O sylvan Wye.'

Wells, Llangammarch Wells and Llanwrtyd Wells brought a new prosperity to the area. Large hotels in each town now aim to provide a range of services for tourists and businesses with restaurants and catering, conference facilities and leisure activities.

Water

Water is one of the area's main assets with many of the largest reservoirs in Britain supplying water to cities and towns across the Midlands and south Wales. Llŷn Brianne, the Elan Valley reservoirs, Nant-y-Moch, Llŷn Clywedog and Lake Vyrnwy were built in the nineteenth and twentieth centuries, changing the landscape forever. They provide vast areas for sporting and leisure facilities such as fishing and sailing with hotels and catering facilities situated in the vicinity.

Forestry

Much of the area was taken over by the Forestry Commission and planting of non-indigenous trees expanded rapidly in the post-war era. Tax concessions in the 1980s saw a big expansion in investment in forestry and a vast acreage of uplands was smothered in pine forest. The benefit to the economy of this activity is no doubt considerable, but the cost to the local environment has been damaging, particularly from the water quality in the numerous streams and rivers that run through the forested areas.

Fir trees cut out light and very little grows beneath them. A walk through any plantation will show this. In addition the acid that comes from the pine leaves makes the run off water poisonous to all insects and invertebrates in the rivers, denying fish their natural feed. Many of the small tributaries of main rivers have become devoid of trout and other fish that used to thrive. These rivers were also the most important spawning grounds for salmon, and the lack of feed now means these cannot support the salmon par. Hence the

Crai Organics produces a range of organically grown gourmet mushrooms from their farm in the Brecon Beacons.

Fly fishing on the upper Wye. The Wye Foundation encourage anglers to return their catch to the river to aid the revival of salmon.

Smoked duck breast from Black Mountains Smokery is served on many menus in the country.

Elan Valley mutton has a rich texture and is busting with flavour. It makes great roasts, casseroles, stew or curry.

number of young salmon returning to the sea has greatly declined.

Wye Foundation

The Wye Foundation has been very active in restoring other spawning grounds within the catchment area. They have improved many small rivers and streams that were hitherto blocked or overgrown to help salmon reach suitable areas. However the River Irfon, once one of the main spawning rivers, remains empty of any life almost to the town of Llanwrtyd Wells.

Grazing

The upland area has endless acres of land suitable for sheep and cattle. The improvement of pasture with land drainage and replanting with grasses opened up many acres of hitherto poor grazing land. The higher ground with natural moor vegetation of heather, mixed grass and weed makes summer grazing for large numbers of sheep that are the main feature of this area.

Organic

The western area of Ceredigion in the Teifi Valley and hinterland from Pumlumon south to Cardigan is lower lying and suitable for mixed farming, with dairy production and crops in abundance. There is a considerable amount of land farmed organically, many following the lead from the success of Rachel's Organic Dairy. The Teifi Valley and the surrounding rolling areas have lush pastures from the abundant rainfall.

The area has some spectacular land forms, particularly the Mynach Falls at Devil's Bridge, at the point where long ago the River Rheidol captured the head waters of the River Teifi, rejuvenating the river to its present dramatic form. Such is the power of the water flow that over the millennia it has cut a deep narrow gorge through the rock to form the famous Punch Bowl.

Mountains

The Cambrian Mountains cover a vast area to the east of the Teifi with much of the area 500 metres above sea level rising to peaks of 650 metres. There is considerable afforestation over higher ground particularly in the upper Irfon Valley and the Abergwesyn Common. Between the land is heath and catchment for tributaries feeding the many reservoirs and main rivers, Tywi and Wye. To the east of the Wye Valley the land of the Radnor Forest north to the Berwyn Mountains is of similar topography with high land reaching 650 metres dissected by the main river of the area the Severn and its many tributaries.

South of the Wye is the vast mountainous area of Mynydd Epynt, the Brecon Beacons and the Black Mountains. The River Usk catchment drains this region which flows eastwards to Abergavenny and then south to the Bristol Channel at Newport. The highest point of the Beacons is over 900 metres, dominating the topography of this southern region. Most of the area is upland heath used for grazing sheep in summer, and extremely popular with mountain walkers throughout the year.

Coastline

The coastline stretches from the Teifi to the Dyfi estuaries which are the two most prominent of the area. Between, smaller rivers mark the fishing harbours that have developed into the popular towns of New Quay and Aberaeron, and the substantial university town Aberystwyth. On the Dyfi is the ancient town of Machynlleth, once the home of Owain Glyndŵr's Welsh Parliament. To this day the town has an air of independence with a large number of privately owned large and small businesses and traders.

Sheep farming is one of the main agricultural activities in the Brecon Beacons. It is estimated that there are about one million sheep in the national park.

Local lamb from Rob Rattray Butchers tastes great when roasted with Welsh rosemary, honey and cider.

Oyster tasting at Aberaeron Seafood Festival, held on the Quay.

Fishing

The area of Cardigan Bay has most fruitful fishing grounds and small fleets of fishing boats operate from Cardigan, New Quay, Aberaeron, Aberystwyth and from some smaller harbours. In the last 50 years the area has attracted much interest from continental fish buyers eager to get hold of the prime catch of the area. Lobster, crab, prawns and scallops have become very valuable catches, their price boosted by continental demand. Regular collections are made from the harbours and large lorries with tanks for holding shellfish, known as vivier lorries, make their way to France and Spain throughout the season.

The area attracts visitors from home and abroad who wish to discover an area generally at a relaxed pace. The numerous attractions include upland walking, mountain biking, adventure four-wheel driving, sea, lake and river angling, water sports such as sailing, waterskiing, canoeing and swimming.

Accommodation

The standard of accommodation and food has improved immensely in the last 20 years, particularly so in the last five. The area now has many luxury country house hotels such as Ynyshir Hall and The Lake Country House that have top international standards. Boutique restaurants with rooms include The Drawing Room and Carlton Riverside. Resort and town accommodation can be to a very high standard with such places as The Harbourmaster (Aberaeron), The Bear (Crickhowell) and The Wynnstay (Machynlleth) receiving high recognition.

Local produce

Many restaurants and pubs have embraced their location and taken to using the local produce from smallholdings, farms, artisan producers, and the inshore fishing fleets. Menus now have the ring of seasonality and freshness with a contemporary approach to cooking and presentation.

menus now have the ring of seasonality and freshness with a contemporary approach to cooking and presentation

Mid Wales: food of the area

The lobster is one of the most beautiful creatures from the sea. Re-stocking programmes and marine conservation areas ensure the species and fishery can be sustained for the future.

Wonderful upland grazing in the Elan Valley, but much of the area has been taken over by the Forestry Commission and dense plantations of conifers cover many acres.

Leafy and green Mid Wales

These central regions have some of the greenest landscapes in Wales; hills, mountains and valleys. The area covers much of the Brecon Beacons and the south-eastern areas of the Snowdonia National Park, the Glyndwr Way and Heritage Coastline. The long sweep of Cardigan Bay has vast fishing grounds used by the inshore fleets based at Aberystwyth, Aberaeron, New Quay, Aberporth and Cardigan and other small sheltered bays and harbours.

Fishing

Trawlers and potting boats fish for lobster, crab, scallops, queens, velvets, prawns, sole, plaice, turbot, brill, monk, bass, cod, mackerel and sewin. Much of the shellfish goes live to the continent with a small amount going to local hotels, restaurants and retailers along with some fresh fish.

Migratory fish

The land is drained by a network of rivers. The Dyfi, Ystwyth, Rheidol and Teifi flow west into Cardigan Bay, whereas the Severn, Wye, and Usk and their tributaries meander eastwards eventually reaching the Bristol Channel. All these rivers are the spawning grounds for migratory salmon that return to their home river when mature to spawn. Rivers flowing into Cardigan Bay also have runs of sewin (sea trout) that have a similar life cycle to the salmon. Large numbers of eels inhabit the rivers and in an opposite cycle to the salmon they return to the Sargasso Sea to breed, returning as tiny elvers to their mother river where they feed and grow for many years. All rivers have significant stocks of resident brown trout and large numbers of coarse fish such as chub, barbel, perch, roach and pike.

In these rivers salmon and sewin are important fisheries regulated by licences for commercial catching and leisure angling. Unfortunately in recent years the catches have declined and very little significant commercial fishing of these species remains, though angling continues on all rivers.

Bottled water

Bottled mineral water is produced by Radnor Hills who have introduced a range of naturally flavoured mineral waters called Heartease that is making a significant mark in this premium market.

Farming

The meat and dairy industries are the main stay of primary food production in the area. Vegetables are produced in most areas on a small scale. There are many organic farms on a relatively small scale in some areas of the Teifi and Usk Valleys and the surrounding area. Welsh lamb is significant everywhere with some areas such as Radnorshire having a name for pasture fed spring lamb. Several major abattoirs are situated in the Teifi Valley and towns such as Llanidloes and Welshpool are centres for distribution and export.

Lamb and beef

The largest producer group in Wales is Meat Promotion Wales/Hybu Cig Cymru, based at Aberystwyth yet promoting red meat from the whole of Wales. Government funding and a levy scheme allows the organisation to work with all meat producers in Wales to maximise their potential at every level of the business.

As throughout Wales, the number of farms specialising in Welsh Black beef has increased. Prime beef production from other breeds, including the expensive Kobe, is also recognised for its quality and provenance. The Burger Manufacturing Company in Builth Wells produces the most wonderful Kobe burgers from the less expensive cuts of this meat.

Organic

An increasing number of farms have converted to or remained organic, farming in the traditional way that was practised

Andrew and Helen Meredith set up Caws Mynydd Du which produces traditional artisan cheeses from sheeps milk including their award-winning Dragons Back cheese.

Welsh Farm Organics provide organic lamb with 100% traceability.

Jonathan Rees surveys the organic pastures on his farm in the rolling hills above Newtown on the Black Mountains.

everywhere until the late 1940s when fertilisers and pesticides came on the scene. The leader of this movement to retain proper farming, i.e.organic, at this time was Dinah Williams and her late husband, the parents of Rachel Rowlands of Rachel's Dairy. For many years Gareth and Rachel Rowlands continued to produce the finest organic milk from the herd of pedigree Guernsey cows selling it to the Milk Marketing Board for precisely the same price as all other farms. Nowadays, Rachel's Dairy is one of the biggest producers of organic milk, yogurt, cream and desserts – and one of the strongest organic brands – in Britain. Everything is made at their state-of-the-art factory in Aberystwyth. Their success has encouraged many other farms across Wales to revert to organic for dairy and meat production.

Meat

Welsh Farm Organics based at Mochdre near Newtown produces organic beef, lamb and pork and sells as much as possible direct to the market via its website. Cambrian Organics is a group of farms doing the same with great success. Graig Farm Organics is one of the most established names in the organic business operating from their farm at Dolau, north of Llandrindod Wells. As well as marketing their own farm produce they have an organic producer group network of farms that market via the Graig Farm banner. This extends into vegetables and seafood all certified to relevant organic standards.

Pigs

Pig farming is part of the agricultural mix and many producers have established reputations for quality ham, bacon and sausages, as well as for fresh pork. The Neuadd Fach Baconry, Pentre Pigs and Pigs' Folley are names to seek in the local shops and markets. The largest producer of sausages is the Welsh Sausage Company of Welshpool owned by Langfords Food Hall.

Their products have been most successful in the national markets with distribution throughout the South East and London.

Cheeses

The Teifi Valley and the surrounding area of the old county of Cardigan has a large amount of dairy farming. Lush pastures give quality pure milk for the processing industry. In this area many of the smaller artisan cheese producers such as Teifi Farmhouse Cheeses, and Trethowan's Dairy have established their names for best quality natural cheese. The former makes Dutch and Continental style cheeses, whereas the latter makes the most traditional Caerphilly. Celtic Promise and Gorwydd from these respective producers have both won major accolades at national and international levels.

Ewe's milk cheese

A promising newer cheesemaker is Caws Mynydd Du, based near Talgarth at the foot of the Black Mountains. In keeping with the name it is made from sheeps' milk from the animals that graze this upland area. It has a distinctive flavour and gives variety to the selection available.

The producer group Cheeses from Wales is based at Ystrad Meurig and represents a significant number of the Welsh cheesemakers situated throughout Wales.

The sparsely spread population of the area does not create centres of demand for some drinks as in North Wales. There are some cider producers close to the English border, notably Ralph's Cider Company. Their distribution is mainly local and at food fairs, but new bottled products are aiming at a wider market. Small vineyards at Aberaeron and Newtown supply to the local market.

Mid Wales: where to eat

Mary Ann Gilchrist in her small kitchen at Carlton Riverside produces wonderfully inspired dishes from local produce from the Irfon Valley.

The Drawing Room has quietly maintained its standards of culinary excellence.

Rack of Welsh lamb is served in restaurants throughout Wales.

● True Taste
Award winners

Barn at Brynich
Baronial barn restaurant specialising in local meats and day boat seafood with rustic presentations allowing produce to speak for itself.
Brynich, Brecon LD3 7SH
T: 01874 623480
www.barn-restaurant.co.uk

Bear Hotel, Crickhowell
This wonderful old coaching hotel retains a true town atmosphere. Here locals and residents mix in the bar to enjoy a drink and a snack or dine in the large flagstoned restaurant which oozes the veritable history of the inn. Prime local ingredients are prepared in well executed dishes whether meat, seafood or game.
High Street, Crickhowell NP8 1BW
T: 01873 810408 E: bearhotel@aol.com
www.bearhotel.co.uk

Carlton Riverside, Llanwrtyd Wells ●
This new restaurant on the bank of the river where it ripples through the small town has one of the finest chefs in the one woman kitchen. The stunningly adept use of ingredients, mainly local, comes through in a series of dishes with techniques and presentations that are original and intriguing. Matching wines and boutique accommodation make this a gem of the Welsh hills.
Irfon Crescent, Llanwrtyd Wells LD5 4RA
T: 01591 610248
E: info@carltonrestaurant.co.uk
www.carltonrestaurant.co.uk

Conrah, Chancery, near Aberystwyth
Fine old Georgian hotel in elevated rural location has spacious well decorated classy rooms.
Chancery, Aberystwyth SY23 4DF
T: 01970 617941
www.conrah.co.uk

Crown, Llwyndafydd
Close to the Ceredigion coastline – serving fresh seafood and local meat.
Llwyndafydd, Llandysul SA44 6BU
T: 01545 560396

Drawing Room, Builth Wells ●
This is one of the most understated fine dining places in Wales. The classic Georgian town house restaurant with rooms has discreet elegance and luxury throughout. The flamboyant menu has many Welsh ingredients from Cardigan to Brecon. Complex dishes have many vegetables, trimmings and sauces all with a purpose to balance flavours and presentation.
Between Cwmbach and Newbridge-on-Wye, Builth Wells LD2 3RT
T: 01982 552493
E: post@the-drawing-room.co.uk
www.the-drawing-room.co.uk

Drovers, Howey near Llandrindod Wells
Asian and eclectic food is an unusual find in this traditional country inn.
Howey, Llandrindod Wells LD1 5PT
T: 01597 822508

Drovers Restaurant, Llanwrtyd Wells
Tea rooms, restaurant and accommodation.
The Square, Llanwrtyd Wells LD5 4RA
T: 01591 610264

Falcondale Hotel, Lampeter
A huge Victorian mansion in many acres of grounds with 'proprietor-cooked food' and rooms of majestic size and décor.
Falcondale Drive, Lampeter SA48 7RX
T: 01570 422910
E: info@falcondalehotel.com
www.falcondalehotel.com

Harbourmaster, Aberaeron

The wonderful setting on the quay makes the most of what is landed by local boats as well as food from the rural area. Light and airy with modern fittings and paintings it's the place to enjoy fresh lobster, crab, prawns scallops and whatever is fresh in season. Local lamb and beef feature alongside the seafood.

Boutique accommodation is of the finest.

Pen Cei, Aberaeron SA46 0BA

T: 01545 570755

E: info@harbour-master.com

www.harbour-master.com

Harp Inn, Old Radnor

This fine old village pub with wonderful country vistas serves honest local food cooked with generosity.

Old Radnor, Presteigne LD8 2RH

T: 01544 350655 E: mail@harpinnradnor.co.uk

www.harpinnradnor.co.uk

Hive on the Quay, Aberaeron ●

Fresh seafood and locally made ice cream – including their signature honey variety – star in this small summer restaurant.

Cadwgan Place, Aberaeron SA46 0BU

T: 01545 570445

E: hiveon.thequay@btinternet.com

www.hiveonthequay.co.uk

Lake Country House, Llangammarch Wells

This fabulous Victorian hotel now has its own new spa and leisure complex. Food in the traditional restaurant takes a very modern approach to combinations and presentations of fine quality produce. Local venison, lamb, beef or perhaps imported tuna all get the chef's flamboyant touch in a series of courses that unravel in a series of flavours. The cavernous wine cellar holds many treasures.

Llangammarch Wells LD4 4BS

T: 01591 620202

E: info@lakecountryhouse.co.uk

www.lakecountryhouse.co.uk

● True Taste
Award winners

Farmers Arms, Cwmdu, near Crickhowell

Friendly local atmosphere and traditional rural fare in a true local inn.

Cwmdu, Crickhowell NP8 1RU

T: 01874 730464

E: cwmdu@aol.com

Felin Fach Griffin

This real gastropub with accommodation has a totally laid back approach in its rural setting. It has been designed for relaxation and enjoyable well prepared food. Much of this hails from the immediate area except the Cornish seafood. The style of the food is that of a London brasserie with careful skill in the cooking and presentation. There is a splendid choice of wine.

Felin Fach, Brecon LD3 0UB

T: 01874 620111

E: enquiries@eatdrinksleep.ltd.uk

www.eatdrinksleep.ltd.uk

Lake Vyrnwy Hotel, Llanwddyn

This large Victorian hotel and restaurant overlooking the reservoir specialises in game from its own estate in winter and caters for lots of visitors in the summer.
Llanwddyn SY10 0LY
T: 01691 870692
E: info@lakevyrnwyhotel.co.uk
www.lakevyrnwy.com

Lasswade, Llangammarch Wells

This small country house hotel presents some well sourced, notable local organic food that personifies this style. Some dishes are quite traditional, some others hit the contemporary style while others hit the contemporary style with items such as caramelized onions, chilli jam and lime couscous making a mark. They come together in a well balanced menu with lots of novel touches right through to the pasteurised Welsh cheeses.

The Felin Fach Griffin is as relaxing as staying in someone's home. Their ethos of the simple things in life done well extends to their menus.

Station Road, Llanwrtyd Wells LD5 4RW
T: 01591 610515 E: info@lasswadehotel.co.uk
www.lasswadehotel.co.uk

Le Vignoble, Aberystwyth

Reasonably priced international cooking from a skilled small team.
31 Eastgate Street, Aberystwyth SY23 2AR
T: 01970 630800

Lion, Llandinam

Convenient pub with rooms serving hearty portions of locally sourced meats.
Llandinam, near Caersws SY17 5BY
T: 01686 688233

Llangoed Hall, Llyswen.

This lovingly restored Clough Williams-Ellis Edwardian mansion has magnificent suites and huge lounges, an art gallery and a billiard room. Many acres of well tended grounds extend to the River Wye. The restaurant aims at modern country house cuisine using much locally sourced meat and Cornish seafood. Service is formal recreating an Edwardian dinner party.
Llyswen, LD3 0YP
T: 01874 754525
E: enquiries@llangoedhall.com
www.llangoedhall.com

Milebrook House

A delightful family-run country house hotel has beautiful rooms and a very good restaurant serving true home-cooked local food of considerable quality, including their own garden vegetables.
Knighton, LD7 1LT
T: 01547 528632
E: hotel@milebrook.kc3ltd.co.uk
www.milebrookhouse.co.uk

Nag's Head Inn, Abercych

Traditional pub with real ales and generous home-cooked food.
Abercych, Boncath SA37 0HJ
T: 01239 841200

Swan at Hay, a charming Regency hotel with all modern comforts and a Gallic-Welsh restaurant menu.

Nantyffin Cider Mill Inn, Crickhowell

This fine old pub adjoins a cider house restaurant.
Brecon Road, Crickhowell NP8 1SG
T: 01873 810775 E: info@cidermill.co.uk
www.cidermill.co.uk

Old Black Lion, Hay-on-Wye

This traditional inn with comfortable rooms serves a big range of bar and restaurant home-cooked food in a characterful ambience.
Lion Street, Hay on-Wye HR3 5AD
T: 01497 820841 E: info@oldblacklion.co.uk
www.oldblacklion.co.uk

The Orangery, Aberystwyth

A modern café wine bar with a bakery and pizzeria serving basic brasserie style dishes, pastries and cakes.
10 Market Street, Aberystwyth SY23 1DL
T: 01970 617606

Peterstone Court, Llanhamlach, near Brecon

The owners have their own farm close-by where they rear a wide range of organic produce including chickens, ducks, guinea fowl, pork, beef and lamb. Cooking is modern yet aims to allow the produce's quality shine whether in a slow roast or a Thai spiced stir-fry. The wine list is an obvious passion. Luxurious bedrooms.
Llanhamlach, near Brecon LD3 7YB
T: 01874 665387
E: enquiries@peterstone-court.com
www.peterstone-court.com

Pilgrim's Tea Rooms, Brecon

Wonderful home-cooked lunches, morning coffee and afternoon tea with beautifully baked savouries and cakes in the cathedral grounds.
Brecon Cathedral, Brecon LD3 9DP
T: 01874 610610
E: enquiries@pilgrims-tearooms.co.uk
www.pilgrims-tearooms.co.uk

River Café, Glasbury

Great riverside bistro with real home cooking.
Glasbury Bridge, Glasbury-on-Wye
HR3 5NP
T: 01497 847007

Seeds, Llanfyllin

Small bistro with home cooking and a wonderful wine list.
5 Penybryn Cottage, High Street, Llanfyllin
SY22 5AP
T: 01691 648604

Stumble Inn, Bwlch-y-Cibau

Hearty pub food in a village pub with real local ambience.
Bwlch-y-Cibau, Llanfyllin SY22 5LL
T: 01691 648860

● True Taste
Award winners

Pristine table
settings at
the Wynnstay
Machynlleth.

Swan at Hay, Hay-on-Wye

This traditional hotel in the internationally
famous town of books has been restored
with a blend of modern and traditional
décor. The food reflects the young chef's
upbringing in the Cote D'Azur.
His treatment of the abundance of prime
ingredients is in sympathy with the local
terroir yet shows the influence of the French
passion for gastronomy.
Church Street, Hay-on-Wye HR3 5DQ
T: 01497 821188 E: info@theswanathay.co.uk
www.swanathay.co.uk

Talkhouse, Pontdolgoch

This is a sophisticated restaurant with
rooms, formerly a coaching inn. In this very
rural setting expect some very fine Welsh
meats and some seafood presented in very
contemporary style.
Pontdolgoch, near Caersws SY17 5JE
T: 01686 688919
www.talkhouse.co.uk

Ultracomida, Aberystwyth ●

This is a stylish café bar in a delicatessen.
The dining is very informal from a snack to
competently cooked full meals.
31 Pier Street, Aberystwyth SY23 2LN
T: 01970 630686

White Swan, Llanfrynach

A great local inn and restaurant with rooms
the cooking is homely using local venison,
lamb and beef with coastal seafood.
Llanfrynach, Brecon LD3 7BZ
T: 01874 665276
www.the-white-swan.com

Wynnstay, Machynlleth

This large dining emporium and comfortable
town hotel has broad offerings for locals,
guests and travellers. It retains its place as the
hub of the community yet specialises in Gallic-
Italian foods. Supreme Welsh ingredients
include game from Dyfi shoots, sea and river
fish, mountain and salt marsh lamb, cooked
in its season. It has traditional pub food, an
Italian pizzeria and Welsh restaurant.
Maengwyn Street, Machynlleth SY20 8AE
T: 01654 702941
E: info@wynnstay-hotel.com
www.wynnstay-hotel.com

Ynyshir Hall, Eglwys Fach

This Georgian country house in rolling
verdant parkland is renowned for its
personal style of décor, ambience and
cuisine. Daily menus aim to give an
experience through the world of gastronomy
with many local ingredients forming the
heart of highly creative dishes. Innovation
appears in every course.
Eglwysfach, near Machynlleth SY20 8TA
T: 01654 781209
E: info@ynyshirhall.co.uk
www.ynyshir-hall.co.uk

Mid Wales: where to buy and producers

The award winning farm shop of Llwynhelyg, stocks a host of local produce much of it grown on their own farm.

Pride in produce – a fine champion bull at the Royal Welsh Show.

Dedicated to the production of cheeses that are produced with unpasteurised milk and committed to retaining traditional cheese making principals.

Country towns

The vast inland areas that cover the Cambrian Mountains, the county of Powys north to the Berwyn Mountains, has just a few towns of any size. There are numerous small villages, many of which are on the old drovers' trails in the valleys and foothills of the mountains.

To the north are the old market towns of Welshpool, Newtown and Machynlleth. In the middle of the area are the Victorian Spa towns of Llandrindod Wells, Builth Wells and Llanwrtyd Wells. To the south is the thriving market town of Brecon, Crickhowell and the border town of Hay-on-Wye. The main area of population on the coast is the university town of Aberystwyth, the very English style Aberaeron, and the former fishing villages of New Quay, Aberporth and Cardigan. The population is otherwise spread very thinly across the area.

Food celebrations

Food festivals celebrate the harvest of the sea at Aberaeron, and the produce of the land at Llanwrtyd Wells and at the Brecon Beacons Food Festival at Libanus. Aberaeron showcases the seafood resources of Wales and has numerous chefs from across Wales demonstrating the use of every conceivable species used in the culinary world. It gives all an opportunity to purchase and stock up with seafood at trawler quay prices.

The Brecon and Llanwrtyd festivals both feature a host of companies from the farming heritage of the area. Expect to find lots of meat, poultry and game, and plenty of organic vegetables from smaller growers of the area. The Llanwrtyd Wells Food Festival is held every spring. Several notable hotels and restaurants – The Lake at Llangammarch, Carlton Riverside and the Lasswade at Llanwrtyd – make this a great weekend destination. The Brecon Beacons Food Festival is held at the Mountain Centre at Libanus every autumn. The centre has an extremely good café restaurant open all

year serving real country cuisine at very reasonable prices, so this show makes an excellent day out.

Local producers

There are many food companies from the area at these festivals. Look for Romy Cuisine pâtés and ready meals that bring a French flavour to best Welsh produce; Pen Pont organic vegetables from their beautiful walled gardens near Brecon; Bacheldre Mill Flour; Caroline's real bread made to traditional time honoured recipes; Brecon Venison reared in natural surroundings in the Beacons; Welsh Black beef and Radnorshire lamb from the Nixon family of Pencae Min near Builth; organic meat from Welsh Farm Organics near Newtown, and Graig Farm Organics of Dolau; Black Mountain Cheese from Talgarth; Crai Organics mushrooms; Brecon Court Wines; organic apple juice from Morris of Crickhowell; Little Cefn homemade conserves; Ralph's Cider and a host of other local food and drinks.

Royal Welsh Show

Every food from land, river and sea is celebrated at this showcase for agriculture and its many related businesses, held at Builth Wells every July. Here the whole of the nation comes together in the most prestigious agricultural show in Britain. The food halls attract producers of every type from all areas of Wales for the four day long bonanza.

The Welsh Winter Fair takes place in the food halls of the showground at the end of November and is a perfect time to stock up and order speciality food, meat and poultry for the Festive Season.

Regular farmers markets are held in Brecon, Llandrindod, Knighton, Presteigne, Llangedwyn, Aberystwyth, Cardigan, Machynlleth and Welshpool. These have become social occasions for many local families and visitors who have become good acquaintances of many of the producers.

Rob Rattray has won a reputation for great quality local produce. Some of the grass-fed lambs are produced on Rob's own farm.

The atmosphere they generate does bring benefits to the regular traders of the area.

Grown on the farm

Farm shops and farm-gate has become the way of shopping for a good segment of the sparse population.

Llwynhelyg Farm Shop, between Aberaeron and Cardigan, attracts regular customers for tempting fresh vegetables from the farm and for homemade foods sourced from small artisan producers. The selection is very comprehensive, covering fresh and cured meat, dairy and bakery foods, pickles and preserves. Others well worth a visit are Wild Carrot near Rhayader, Pig's Folly at Garth Mill, the Welsh Venison Centre at Bwlch and Graig Farm at Dolau.

Specialists

Many independent butchers find that diversifying into fine foods enables their family businesses to thrive. A notable example is Langford's Food Hall in Welshpool. This was a family butchers of note but has expanded into a 'must-visit' food shop. An associated business,

The Welsh Sausage Company, supplies major outlets across the UK. On a more modest scale, other independent butchers well worth a visit include W J George of Talgarth, Julian Roberts of Builth Wells, Rob Rattray of Aberystwyth, William Lloyd Williams of Machynlleth and Ricki Lloyd of Welshpool, along with many other local butchers.

Independent specialist shops and delicatessens of note are holding their own in the market. Ultracomida in Aberystwyth has a wonderful range of international produce and the best of Welsh specialities, plus a sophisticated restaurant. Also check out The Treehouse. In Machynlleth visit Blasau Delicatessen and Quarry Wholefoods, and the Mulberry Bush in Lampeter. Both M T Cashell and Granville's in Crickhowell stock many local foods. For fresh fish visit Fish on the Quay in Aberaeron. In New Quay the Honey Farm is a delightful experience for high tea and to see the process of honey making and its uses from producing beeswax to mead.

Caws Cymru

Throughout the area, most towns have a local Spar shop, many of which stock quality Welsh foods such as dry-cured bacon from the Neuadd Fach Baconry in Llandinam, made entirely from their own free-range pigs. Caws Cymru of Pentregat supply a full range of Welsh farmhouse cheeses, chutneys, canned laverbread and artisan foods from many small companies to the Spar and other independent shops in the area.

Online

For many, sourcing the rich produce of this area is difficult, but in the twenty-first century there are some producers with excellent websites from which anyone in the country can purchase for the following-day delivery. Welsh Farm Organics, Graig Farm and Cambrian Hills Company have geared themselves for this market and shopping with them can be done from an armchair.

True Taste
Award winners

Artisan millers
of exceptional
flours. Bacheldre
Watermill use
traditional milling
equipment,
some of which is
hundreds of
years old.

markets, shops, specialists and producers in Mid Wales

Bacheldre Watermill

Stoneground flour and bread mixes.
Churchstoke, Montgomery SY15 6TE
T: 01588 620489
E: info@bacheldremill.co.uk
www.bacheldremill.co.uk

Black Mountains Smokery

Cold and hot smoked fish, meat and poultry.
Leslie House, Elvicta Business Park,
Crickhowell NP8 1DF
T: 01873 811566 E: admin@smoked-foods.co.uk
www.smoked-foods.co.uk

Blasau Delicatessen

Local meat, vegetables, cheeses and eggs.
6 Penrallt Street, Machynlleth SY20 8AJ
T: 01654 700410

Brecon Market

Town market with traditional producers
and retailers.
Market Hall, Brecon LD3 9BU
T: 0845 6076060

Burger Manufacturing Company

Quality burgers from Welsh meats and
Kobe beef.
Wyeside Enterprise Park, Builth Wells
LD2 3UA
T: 01982 551713
E: john@qualityburgers.co.uk
www.qualityburgers.co.uk

Caermynydd Piggery

Free-range pork, sausages and cured bacon
and ham.
Caermynydd, Penuwch SY25 6RF
T: 01974 821361
www.caermynydd-piggery.co.uk

Caroline's Real Bread Company

Artisan styles cover a wide range of
baking culture.
The Old Vicarage, Merthyr Cynog,
Brecon LD3 9SD
T: 01874 690378
E: carolinesrealbread@virgin.net

Castle Kitchen

Healthy eating menu in the café and the
shop speaks of local food.
Broad Street, Montgomery SY15 6PH
T: 01686 668795

Caws Celtica

Ewes' milk hard mature cheese.
Capel Gwnda, Rhydlewis, near Llandysul
SA44 5RN
T: 01239 851419
E: info@cawsceltica-farmhousecheese.co.uk
www.cawsceltica-farmhousecheese.co.uk

True Taste
Award winners

Caws Cymru

Wholesalers of Welsh cheeses and
specialist produce.
Unit 1, Wervil Grange, Pentregat
near Llandysul SA44 6HW
T: 01239 654800

Caws Mynydd Du ◉

Ewes' milk cheese, cheddar style.
Lodge Farm, Talgarth, Brecon LD3 0DP
T: 01874 711812
www.cawsmyndddu.com

Charlie Hicks

Specialist vegetable dealer and shop.
22 Castle Street, Hay-on-Wye HR3 5DF
T: 01497 822742
E: enquiries@charliehicks.com
www.charliehicks.com

Cheeses From Wales

Producer group for marketing Welsh cheese.
Tyn-y Llwyn, Pontrhydygroes,
Ystrad Meurig SY25 6DP
T: 01974 282572
E: sales@cheesesfromwales.com
www.cheesesfromwales.com

Chef on the Run Foods

Preserves, jams, chutney, mustard.
The Old Stables Tea Rooms, Bear Street,
Hay-on-Wye HR3 5AN
T: 01497 821557
E: info@chefontherunfoods.co.uk
www.chefontherunfoods.co.uk

Cig Oen Caron

Welsh meat abattoir and wholesaler.
The Abattoir, Tregaron, SY25 6JL
T: 01974 298964

Clam's Handmade Cakes ◉

Traditional Welsh recipes for homemade
style cakes.
Unit 49 Elvicta Business Park, Crickhowell
NP8 1DF
T: 01873 812283
www.clamscakes.co.uk

Crai Organics ◉

Specialist mushrooms including shitake and
oyster mushrooms.
Glwydcaenewydd Farm, Crai, near
Sennybridge LD3 8YP
T: 01874 638973

Dunbia

Large dealer and abattoir for Welsh meats
from the Teifi Valley and surrounding
regions.
Teifi Park, Lampeter Road, Llanybydder
SA40 9QE
T: 01570 480284
www.dungannonmeats.com

Elan Valley Mutton Co ◉

True mutton specialists – farm shop,
and online purchases.
Henfron, Elan Valley, Rhayader LD6 5HE
T: 01597 811240
www.elanvalleymutton.co.uk

Face of Flowers

Organic meat, poultry and vegetables on line
and from warehouse.
Lampeter Business Park, Lampeter
SA48 8LT
T: 01570 423523
E: enquires@face-of-flowers-organic.co.uk
www.face-of-flowers-organic.co.uk

Feast of Food

Delicatessen with many local foods.
2 Station Road, Caersws SY17 5EQ
T: 01686 689149

Fish On The Quay

Locally landed fish direct from boats
in season.
Caedwgan Place, Aberaeron SA46 0BUT:
01545 570599

G J Morris Organic Apple Juice ◉

Freshly pressed organic apple juice.
Graig Barn Farm, Llangenny Lane,
Crickhowell NP8 1HB
T: 01873 810275

Graig Farm Organics
Organic farm meats, poultry, vegetables, preserves and seafoods all from accredited sources.
Dolau, Llandrindod Wells LD1 5TL
T: 01597 851655
E: sales@graigfarm.co.uk
www.graigfarm.co.uk

Gwinllan Ffynnon Las Vineyard
White and rosé wines from coastal vineyard.
Ffynnon Las, Aberaeron SA46 0ED
T: 01545 570234
E: martin.lewis@ffynnon-las.co.uk
www.ffynnon-las.co.uk

Hamer International
Wholesale lamb and beef throughout Wales and internationally.
Dolwen, Oakley Park, Llanidloes SY18 6LX
T: 01686 412114
E: hamer.sales@lineone.net

Irfon Valley Lamb
Town butchers shop specialising in local lamb and farm-assured meats.
Abernant Shop, Llanwrtyd Wells LD5 4RA
T: 01938 556890
E: info@irfonvalleylamb.co.uk
www.irfonvalleylamb.co.uk

Knobbly Carrot Food Company
Organic vegetables products – soups and sandwich fillings.
Unit 18, Lampeter Buisness Park, Lampeter SA48 8LT
T: 01570 422064
sales@theknobblycarrot.co.uk
www.theknobblycarrot.co.uk

Langfords Food Hall
Master butcher's shop and impressive food hall with copious local produce.
4 Berriew Street, Welshpool SY21 75Q
T: 01938 552331
E: john@langfords-foodhall.co.uk
www.langfords-foodhall.co.uk

Llanllyr Water Company
Llanllyr Source comes from beneath certified organic fields on the Llanllyr Farm in West Wales.
Talsarn, Lampeter SA48 8QB
T: 01570 470788
E: sales@llanllyrwater.com
www.llanllyrwater.com

Llwynhelyg Farm Shop
Wonderful homegrown produce picked every day in season.
Llwynhelyg, Sarnau, Llandysul SA44 6QU
T: 01239 811079
E: llwynhelygfarmshop@ukonline.co.uk
www.llwynhelygfarmshop.co.uk

Merlin Cheeses
Hard goats' milk cheddar style cheese.
Tyn-y Llwyn, Pontrhydygroes, Ystrad Meurig SY25 6DP
T: 01974 282636
E: merlincheeses@tiscali.co.uk

Mulberry Bush
Delicatessen and local produce shop.
2 Bridge Street, Lampeter SA48 7HG
T: 01570 423317
www.mulberrywholefoods.co.uk

Nantclyd Organics
Eggs, vegetables and fruit from the farm gate.
Llanilar, Aberystwyth SY23 4SL
T: 01974 241543
E: liz@nantclydorganics.co.uk
www.nantclydorganics.co.uk

Neuadd Fach Baconry
Cured bacon and sausages and hams from own farm pigs.
Neuadd Fach, Llandinam SY17 5AS
T: 01686 688734
E: Lynda@baconry.co.uk
www.baconry.co.uk

New Quay Honey Farm

Live beehives, honey, mead, candles
and café.
Cross Inn, New Quay SA44 6NN
T: 01545 560822
E: enquires@thehoneyfarm.co.uk
www.thehoneyfarm.co.uk

Organic Fresh Foods Company

Wholesaler of organic vegetables.
Unit 25, Lampeter Industrial Estate,
Lampeter SA48 8LT
T: 01570 424424
E: enquires@organicfarmfoods.co.uk
www.organicfreshfoodcompany.co.uk

Organic Smokehouse

All produce is from organic sources,
cured and smoked to exacting standards.
Oak Meadow, Bacheldre, Church Stoke,
Montgomery SY15 6TE
T: 01588 660206
E: info@organicsmokehouse.com
www.organicsmokehouse.com

Penarth Vineyard Estate

White and rosé wines from extensive
vineyards.
Pool Road, Newtown SY16 3AN
T: 01686 610383
E: info@penarthvineyard.co.uk
www.penarthvineyard.co.uk

Pencrugiau Organic Farm Shop

Organic vegetables, herbs and salad boxes.
Pencrugiau, Felindre Farchog, Crymych
SA41 3XH
T: 01239 881265

Penmincae Welsh Black Beef & Lamb

Farm-reared pedigree Welsh Black beef
and lamb.
Genllynen Lodge, Cwmbach, Llechrhyd,
Builth Wells LD2 3RP
T: 01982 551242

Penpont Organic

Vegetables, fruit and salads from walled
gardens.
Penpont Estate, Brecon LD3 8EU
T: 01874 636202
www.penpont.com

Pentre Pigs

Consultancy in pig rearing and butchery.
Pentre House, Leighton, Welshpool
SY21 8HL
T: 01938 553430
E: enquires@pentrepigs.co.uk
www.pentrepigs.co.uk

Pigs Folly Shop

Homemade sausages in numerous flavours.
New Inn, Newbridge-on-Wye, Llandrindod
Wells LD1 6HY
T: 01597 860211
www.pigsfolly.co.uk

Rachel's Organic Dairy

Organic yogurt and other dairy produce
– the leading organic brand.
Unit 63, Glanyrafon, Aberystwyth SY23 3JQ
T: 01970 625805
E: enqs@rachelsorganic.co.uk
www.rachelsorganic.co.uk

Radnor Hills Mineral Water

Naturally flavoured sparkling water,
Heartsease.
Knighton LD7 1LU
T: 01547 530220
E: sales@radnorhills.co.uk
www.radnorhills.com

Ralph's Cider and Perry

Artisan farmhouse cider and perry,
natural and sparkling.
Old Badland Farm, New Radnor,
Presteigne LD8 2TG
T: james@ralphscider.co.uk
www.ralphsciderfestival.co.uk

Rob Rattray Butchers ◉

Traditional butchers supplying locally produced meats including award-winning home cured bacon, sausages, cooked meats and pies.
8 Chalybeate Street, Aberystwyth
SY23 1HS
T: 01970 615353

Romy Cuisine

French style pâtés and dishes all from Welsh ingredients.
PO Box 106, Hay-on-Wye HR3 5YH
T: 07855 531550
E: info@romycuisine.co.uk
www.romycuisine.co.uk

Teifi Farmhouse Cheese ◉

Raw milk cheese, unpasteurised washed rind and continental styles.
Glynhynod, Ffostrasol, near Llandysul
SA44 5JY
T: 01239 851528

Treehouse

Organic shop with meat, vegetables and groceries, restaurant with organic cooking.
14 Baker Street, Aberystwyth SY23 2BJ
T: 01970 615791
E: info@treehousewales.co.uk
www.treehousewales.co.uk

Trethowan's Gorwydd Caerphilly ◉

Mature farmhouse Caerphilly cheese handmade using traditional rennet and unpasteurised cows milk
Gorwydd Farm, Llanddewi Brefi,
Tregaron SY25 6NY
T: 01570 493 516

Ultracomida Delicatessen

Traditional and modern style delicatessen
31 Pier Street, Aberystwyth SY23 2LN
T: 01970 630686

Welsh Farm Organics ◉

Organic farm meats – Welsh lamb, beef and pork, cured and cooked products.
Tyn y Fron, Mochdre, Newtown SY16 4JW
T: 07855 311740
E: sales@welshfarmorganics.co.uk
www.welshfarmorganics.co.uk

Welsh Sausage Company

Top quality sausages for retail and catering nationwide.
Greenfields, Foundry Lane,
Welshpool SY21 7AW
T: 01938 553365
E: john@langfords-foodhall.co.uk
www.langfords-foodhall.co.uk

Welsh Venison Centre

Free-range farmed venison, butchered and sold directly from shop.
Middlewood Farm, Bwlch, Brecon LD3 7HQ
T: 01874 730929
E: welshvenison@btconnect.com
www.welshvenisoncentre.co.uk

Wild Carrot

Organic farm shop with vegetables, fruit, bread, dairy and eggs.
Allt Goch Farm, St Harmon, Rhayader
LD6 5LG
T: 01597 870273

William Lloyd Williams & Sons

Quality butcher – fine local lamb and beef.
5 – 7 Maengwyn Street, Machynlleth
SY20 8AA
T: 01654 702106
E: wil-lloyd@fsmail.net
www.wil-lloyd.co.uk

W J George

Traditional butcher with local meats from own abattoir.
Cross House, High Street, Talgarth,
Brecon LD3 0PD
T: 01874 711233
E: sales@talgarthmeat.com
www.talgarthmeat.com

south West Wales

The fertile meadow
land surrounding
Weobley Castle.

South West Wales

Pembrokeshire has its dramatic coastal walk, the Preseli hills, tranquil St Davids and the magnificent Milford Haven waterway. Carmarthenshire's fertile Tywi Valley contrasts with industrial Glamorgan to the east. Dylan Thomas's "ugly, lovely town" of Swansea has the scenic gem of Gower on its doorstep. Sustainable fisheries and seasonal crops – along with lamb, beef and dairy products from rich pasture – ensure that market produce glistens with freshness.

Fishguard
Newport
Llandovery
Porthgain
St David's
Llandeilo
Solva
Haverfordwest
Carmarthen
Broad Haven
Narberth
Laugharne
Saundersfoot
Pembroke
Tenby
Swansea
Reynoldston
Mumbles

South West Wales: about the area

The rugged coast of Pembrokeshire is bathed by the temperate waters of the Gulf Stream that keeps the climate mild giving a long growing season for crops.

The waters of the Bristol Channel are rich fishing grounds for bass and many other species.

Premier county

Pembrokeshire, the oldest county in Wales, is known as the Premier County. It forms the western part of this region, which also takes in Carmarthenshire and the area once known as West Glamorgan. The long coastline extends from the Teifi to the Afan Estuary, taking in the outstandingly beautiful Pembrokeshire coast, Carmarthen Bay, Gower Peninsula and Swansea Bay.

The area has some of the most prime agricultural land in Britain. The coast is bathed by the Gulf Stream that maintains an equable climate throughout the year. South Pembrokeshire and Gower are relatively frost free enabling a very long growing season. The green land extends across Carmarthenshire and into West Glamorgan where the industrial landscape begins.

Coalfields

A significant part of the South Wales coalfield extends to the west of Llanelli where some of the last modern mines were sited. In this area both steel and coal industries dominated the economy throughout the nineteenth and twentieth centuries. Many of the smelters and mills have closed and the land has been redeveloped as business parks or returned to nature. The National Wetland Centre Wales, near Llanelli, is on the former site of a steelworks that closed in the 1980s.

Industry

The lower Swansea Valley has now largely been cleared of industrial spoil and modern business parks put in its place. The remaining steelworks at Margam in Port Talbot is the last sign of the great industrial heritage of the area. Swansea Valley was the non-ferrous metal centre of the world. The remaining plants in the area are the Mond Nickel works at Clydach and Alcoa Aluminium at Waunarlwydd. Coal mining is all but a shadow of a by-gone era that once dominated the landscape. Modern mines in the upper Neath Valley typify today's production of coal, with minimal scar on the landscape.

The areas that once housed heavy industry are now packed with modern industrial estates. High technology companies have moved in at a pace, and many food production and distribution companies are located on these estates. It all adds to the clean and green image that modern industry seeks to portray.

Much of the area is open countryside, either farmland or upland, that makes a significant contribution to the economy. The county of Pembrokeshire has some of the richest agricultural land in Britain, as well as a coastline suitable for a wide range of activities.

Harbours

Milford Haven is one of the greatest natural harbours in the world and was recognised as such by Lord Nelson. Its strategic position in times of war was of great importance. Naval shipbuilding yards and munitions factories were located there. Since the Second World War, it has become a major centre of the oil industry, with deep-water access for supertankers supplying oil refineries situated alongside the quays. Initial developments aimed to blend with the landscape but as activity increased so this element decreased. More recent developments include a new natural gas terminal and distribution network and power stations.

The fishing fleet at Milford Docks declined steadily in the post-war era. What was the major western port for hake fishing has all but disappeared. It now houses foreign-registered super trawlers that land their catch directly for foreign markets. A number of locally based boats land a variety of prime fish.

The Haven now has several marinas for the leisure boating industry and this has made a major contribution to the economy,

The sheltered natural harbour of Porthclais.

particularly all the associated service and catering industries. Ferries operate between Pembroke and Ireland bring a year-round flow of business and commerce.

Land

Most of the county is prime agricultural land around 70 metres above sea level. Similar to Gower the southern area is carboniferous limestone covered with glacial from the Ice Age. With the warming influence of the Gulf stream the climate is mild in winter and enables a long growing season for crops. The county is renowned for early potatoes and subsequent crops of greens and roots, asparagus and summer fruit. The area north of the Haven and the market town of Haverfordwest is prime traditional mixed farming land. It then rises to the Preseli Hills some 500 metres above sea level where the land is typical upland heath with heather and bracken mainly suitable for grazing sheep.

Coast

The Pembrokeshire Coastal Path National Trail extends for 179 miles (288km), taking in some of Wales's finest scenery. It's virtually undisturbed by man but for a few places where granite quarrying in the nineteenth century made its mark. Endless miles of gull and raven haunted cliffs have numerous small harbours that give shelter to the coastal fishing fleet. Fishguard Bay is the major ferry port for Ireland and has a large naturally sheltered mooring for many other fishing and leisure craft. There are tiny harbours in old quarrying areas such as Porthgain and Abereiddy.

On the western extreme is the smallest City in Britain and the beautiful cathedral of St Davids set in a strategic position hidden in a valley invisible to maritime invaders. Constructed from purple stone quarried from the cliffs of nearby Caerfai Bay and with an Irish oak roof it is a true gem of architecture and a haven of tranquillity.

Fishermen land their catch everyday so you will find a variety of fresh fish and shellfish on menus across the region.

Welsh farmhouse cheese truckles maturing on wooden shelves. Each has to be turned every few days for many months while it matures.

A few miles offshore is the island of Ramsey and beyond a string of smaller ones called the Bishops and Clerks, some no more than bare rocks serving as a vantage post for fishing cormorants.

Islands

The island of Skomer sits off the southern tip of St Brides Bay. Puffins, razorbills, Manx shearwaters, peregrine falcons and short-eared owls are amongst the host of birds that inhabit this island. It's now a National Nature Reserve and marine sanctuary. It can be reached from Martin's Haven on the *Dale Princess* that operates daily excursions from April to October. The southern coast has a string of small islands such as Sheep Island and Crow Rock and the monastic Caldey Island, home to a community of Cistercian monks.

Carmarthenshire

The county of Carmarthenshire extends from the estuary of the rivers Tâf, Tywi and Gwendraeth as far north as Llŷn Brianne high in the Cambrian Mountains in the upper reaches of the River Tywi. Dyffryn Tywi, the Vale of Tywi, extends from the county market town of Carmarthen to Llandovery and over the Sugar Loaf Mountain to Llanwrtyd Wells, the smallest town in Britain. It takes in the Black Mountain between the upper Swansea and Tywi Valleys, actually the western part of the Brecon Beacons.

The coastline is a stretch of planar sands separated by the rivers Tâf, Tywi and Gwendraeth. The four-mile stretch at Pendine was the location of several land-speed record attempts where Malcolm Campbell and Parry Thomas battled for supremacy in the 1920s. The eastern sands beyond Kidwelly were taken over by the military for practice manoeuvres.

The undulating land is prime dairy country and mixed farming. Carmarthen Bay is a favoured ground for fishing trawlers that catch a wide range of prime species. The rivers of the county, the Tywi, Cothi, Tâf and Kidwelly are renowned for salmon and sewin, while the sands of the estuaries are targets for cockle pickers from far and wide.

Gower

The eastern part of the area takes in the Gower Peninsula, Britain's first designated Area of Outstanding Natural Beauty. The carboniferous limestone cliffs of the southern coast have numerous caves and fossils with evidence of human habitation back to Neolithic times. The 'Red Lady' of Paviland cave was the oldest skeleton discovered when it was unearthed in the 1920s.

Much of the land is rich and fertile and the mild climate is similar to Pembrokeshire. The north Gower coast is almost entirely salt marsh from Whiteford Burrows to Loughor providing thousands of acres of grazing for sheep in summer.

Carmarthen ham is dry cured ham similar to that from Bayonne or Parma and is the speciality of Albert Rees' stall in Carmarthen Market.

Haverfordwest Market was voted Famers' Market of the Year 2006 for its positive overall market performance, sustainability and impact on community, farming and the public.

Worm's Head, viewed here from Rhossili Downs, extends a mile into the Atlantic Ocean. Sunsets here are said to be one of the top 10 of all magnificent sunsets in the world.

Beyond are the famous cockle beds that have been fished commercially for several centuries.

The south coast is a series of rocky headlands and sandy bays of truly breathtaking beauty. On the extreme south west is Worm's Head, itself a peninsula reaching out a mile into the ocean. The sunsets here are said to be one of the 10 greatest in the world. Rhossili Bay is a three-mile sweep of golden sand accessible only by footpaths. Further east, several smaller beaches Tor Bay, Three Cliffs Bay and Pobbles Bay are wonderfully secluded and tranquil. Similarly, Pwll Du is a secret hidden cove. Caswell and Langland have car parks and are popular with day trippers.

Swansea

The City of Swansea has seen much development in the last decade. The city centre, the marina and the new SA1 dockland development have revitalised the economy, attracting modern businesses and tourism. The Swansea and Neath Valleys now have several business parks and housing developments on land that has been reclaimed after several centuries of industrial activity. The rivers are now clean and have natural stocks of fish, including migratory salmon and sewin. The surrounding valleys and hills are covered with vegetation and home to livestock in places where coal tips dominated the scene until 20 years ago.

Tourists

Tourism is now a major source of income for the economy. Proximity to the conurbations of the M4 corridor makes the area easily accessible. Tourist attractions are in every town and city, with culture and entertainment everywhere along with numerous outdoor pursuits. The must-sees in the area are Gower, Milford Haven waterway, Skomer island and St Davids. Food attractions are numerous starting with Swansea Market, the largest indoor market in Wales. Carmarthen Market has wonderful local produce and the best farmers' market is in Haverfordwest. There are numerous small and larger farm shops, delicatessens and general stores that stock produce of the area including seafood, vegetables, meat, artisan cheeses, chutneys and preserves.

Food

The catering industry, as in the North Wales area, has improved out of all recognition and it is possible to find good food with empathy for the area in most places. Swansea and Gower have many places including some of the finest boutique hotels and restaurants with rooms in the area. Pembroke has always been renowned for top quality produce and many restaurants and hotels have embraced this on menus.

St Davids has a large number of recognised restaurants for the smallest city in Britain, including a restaurant in the refectory of the cathedral itself. Newport has become a centre of gastronomy with several restaurants, hotels and gastro pubs in the small area. In Pembrokeshire there are still some nicely quirky places untouched by fashion and trends, except perhaps for the welcome trend to serve food that is locally sourced.

South West Wales: food of the area

Lobsters are landed regularly from fishermen in South West Wales.

A fine hen crab taken from a pot off the Pembrokeshire coast – to be turned into delicious dressed crab by Dash Shellfish in Little Haven.

This relatively small area is south of the Teifi and Llyn Brianne taking in Pembrokeshire, Carmarthenshire, Gower and Swansea. It is the most significant food producing area of all of Wales for its richness and diversity and proximity to the major market of South East Wales with links directly to the Midlands, South East England and London markets.

The area has a mix of industry and agriculture, and their associated businesses, plus fishing and coastal harvesting. The traditional coal, iron and steel industries of Llanelli, Swansea, Neath and Port Talbot and associated trading created large centres of population in close proximity to this major food producing area. The oil industry has created a vibrant economy in Pembrokeshire in addition to the agricultural base.

Fishing

The coastline of Pembrokeshire has many miles of fine fishing grounds. Numerous small fleets of boats operate from Fishguard, St Davids, Solva, Tenby and Milford Haven and other fine quays such as Porthgain, Abereiddy, Martin's Haven and Stackpole. The large fishing boats that operate from Milford using hefty beam trawls are mainly foreign registered and the catch goes directly to continental markets. Prime fish such as Dover Sole, turbot, plaice, monk and bass fetch high prices and agents have computer links with all these markets.

The numerous creel fishing boats and smaller trawlers catch crab, lobster, spider crabs, velvets and crayfish most of which disappear in vivier lorries to the Continent. Many small boats line fish for bass that is always in demand. Mackerel is very plentiful over the summer caught by small commercial and leisure boats. There is a similar small inshore fishery based in Swansea and Mumbles operating around the Gower coast and in the Bristol Channel as far as Lundy Island.

Herring

The winter herring fishery in the Haven yields large landings particularly where the fish accumulate on the Cleddau Estuary at Llangwm. These were the mainstay of the inshore winter fishery and many were made into kippers and bloaters in the curing houses of the fish docks at Milford.

Salmon and Sewin

The estuary of the Three Rivers, the Tâf, Tywi and Gwendraeth is the most productive commercial fishery for salmon and sewin regulated by licences. In the past small boats based at Ferryside using long floating nets could catch lucrative quantities of these fish in the season, plus bass, mullet and flounders as a by-catch. A similar fishery at Cardigan on the Teifi has seen the same slow decline. Further up these rivers traditional coracles were used to tow the nets to trap salmon and sewin. A few people still fish by this method but basically for pleasure rather than commercial level.

Cockles

The Three Rivers and the Loughor Estuary have commercial stocks of cockles that can be raked from the sands at low tide when hundreds of acres of cockle beds are exposed. The centre of the fishery is at Penclawdd in North Gower. Here the fishery is regulated by licences that control the method of gathering and quantity harvested over the year. Large commercial cockle-dredging boats used in other areas of Britain are not permitted. This has enabled the fishery to continue and maintain commercial stocks. It is the first fishery of its type to be accredited by the Marine Stewardship Council as a sustainable fishery. Commercial stocks of cockles are present in the other uncontrolled parts of the Three Rivers but competition between rival groups of pickers can lead to much controversy.

Small trawlers and lobster boats fish Swansea Bay and the Bristol Channel landing their catch daily.

Beetroot is now a popular vegetable in restaurants.

Organic pannacotta with passion fruit and caramelised bananas.

Penclawdd cockles and laverbread are specialities of Swansea Market.

Laverbread

The cockle producers of Penclawdd also cook laverbread as a second product to sell in the markets. This seaweed, gathered around the coast of Gower and Pembrokeshire, and also as far as Llŷn or even Scotland, is sent to Penclawdd for processing. In the past most of the 30 or so families cooking cockles also produced laverbread. Now three companies prepare laverbread on a commercial scale.

Dairy

The productive land of Carmarthenshire, Pembrokeshire and Gower is prime for traditional mixed farming. The area is renowned for its dairy produce, vegetables, Welsh lamb, beef, pork and poultry. The abundance of these foods from the land can be seen in Carmarthen and Swansea Markets.

The introduction of milk quotas changed the farming scene for many and 20 years on the industry has re-shaped. Several of the large creameries have disappeared while smaller producers and producer groups have emerged. A classic is the Calon Wen organic co-operative based in the heart of dairy country at Whitland. They are marketing the message of organic and sustainable not only in their product but packaging as well, promoting themselves directly to consumers in the multiples.

Cheese

Specialist small scale and artisan cheese making has developed alongside the larger producers a result of milk quotas that made many look for some form of value added to their farm production. Caws Cenarth at Boncath have been leaders originally making traditional Caerphilly. Now they have a range of soft brie style cheeses and a medium soft blue making a trio of styles for a cheese board. Other specialists include Llanboidy Farmhouse Cheeses, Nantybwla Farm Cheeses, Caerfai, and the newer Carmarthenshire Cheese Company who

have a range of soft and cheddar styles. In the Preseli Mountains Pant Mawr Farm make a range of soft, and smoked cheeses. Cothi Valley Goats at Talley produce one of the best ranges of artisan soft and hard goats' cheeses in Britain and is well known in farmers' markets throughout southern Britain and London.

Vegetables

The mild climate of the South West means that produce can be grown over a long season. In Gower two crops can be harvested in one season and like south Pembroke the area is well suited to early new potatoes. Before the influx of imports from around the globe these could be a bonanza for the growers who could capitalise on high early season prices. Through the year the crops cover a wide range including cauliflowers, leeks, cabbages, beans, asparagus, lettuce, soft fruits and root vegetables.

Meat

Both lamb and beef are important in the mixed farming economy. Welsh lamb is reared in the entire region from the higher land of the Preseli Mountains and Cambrian Mountains down to the coastal fringe. Salt marsh lamb has been a more recent discovery as a premium product. The tidal estuaries of the Three Rivers and Loughor have acres of summer grazing with the marshes of Laugharne and Llanrhidian as the main areas. Through the season this is becoming most popular on menus in local restaurants and throughout the country distributed by specialist suppliers.

There are numerous farms specialising in beef production from a range of British and Continental breeds. Welsh Black has become more popular as in other regions. Several organic farms have made their mark in the industry and marketed the breed at a premium to caterers in major cities. Companies such as Welsh Hook Meats, Celtic Pride, Fferm Tyllwyd,

Harmony Herd in the Teifi Valley has wild boar and rare-breed pigs. Their produce is in most farmers' markets across South Wales.

A number of artisan preserve companies, such as Miranda's Preserves and Wendy Brandon Handmade Preserves, make use of the abundance of soft fruit in the area.

Hurn's brand of Tomos Watkins ales and beers, such as Cwrw Hâf and Cwrw Braf, are sold in supermarkets, pubs and restaurants.

Hops and barley make a fine brew of real ale at the Hurns Brewery.

Bethesda Farm Meats and Welsh Quality Meats have been active in promoting Welsh meats to a wide market.

Pembroke Turkeys are considered as special for the Christmas market. There are no mass producers as in East Anglia, but a handful of smaller farms with free-range flocks such as Caermelyn Turkeys and Welsh Haven Foods. Many smaller farms produce free-range chickens and eggs.

Butchers

Pigs are very much a part of the mixed farming economy. Traditionally every farm kept some pigs as the staple food. Curing hams and bacon, making sausages, faggots, black pudding, brawn and chitterlings is the Welsh equivalent of Continental charcuterie. All the markets and local butchers have a range of these products, many homemade in the shop kitchen. Some are specialising in their products such as Felinfoel Faggots and Albert Rees' Carmarthen Ham, and Pembrokeshire Pork and Sausage Company. Harmony Herd, Newcastle Emlyn produce wild boar and rare breeds on their organic farm. They cure beacon and hams and make sausages to sell in local markets.

Water

Several notable companies have set up to produce bottled mineral and spring water from their natural source. Brecon Carreg Water comes from the Black Mountain close to the historic Carreg Cennen Castle. Tŷ Nant has been the most successful with its stylish presentation that is seen on top tables throughout the world.

Breweries

In the coal mining era many breweries set up to cater for the demand from the expanding population of miners. Buckley's, Felinfoel, Hancock's and Vale of Neath Breweries catered for this mass market. In recent years specialists have set up to cater for the revived market for cask conditioned and premium bottled ales. Hurns Brewing Company and Evan-Evans are well established in this market.

Preserves

In this rich food-producing area of South West Wales many bespoke companies have set up making a range of products including chutneys, preserves, jams and confectionery. There are many bakeries producing bread, cakes, sweet and savoury pies, tarts and flans for the large markets in the major towns of the area. The large local market has encouraged development of seafood processing, organic vegetable products, and ready meals for the food service industry. Many of these companies are dependent on the distribution of their products by the leading merchant for Welsh food products Castell Howell based in Carmarthen. The company operates a fleet of vans distributing to caterers and retailers throughout Wales and beyond and also has a cash and carry at their depot.

The wide range of products available and a distribution network based in the regions enables numerous shops and caterers to have access to local produce with very low food miles.

numerous shops and caterers have access to local produce with very low food miles

south West Wales: where to eat

At Fairyhill the cuisine is informed, accurate and makes good use of the natural produce from the Gower Peninsula.

Y Polyn is a simple country pub with great food owned by Sue and Mark Manson (pictured) and Maryann and Simon Wright.

The Shed serves the freshest fish and shellfish - straight from the sea and onto the table.

Angel Inn & Capel Bach Bistro, Llandeilo

Great town bistro serving good value local food.
62 Rhosmaen Street, Llandeilo SA19 6EN
T: 01558 822765
E: paul@angelbistro.co.uk
www.angelbistro.co.uk

Angel, Salem

This restaurant in its rural setting serves some of the most sophisticated cuisine in Wales. The style takes in the classical yet comes into the most modern in skillful combinations of masterful gastronomy. Treatment of meat, seafood and vegetables is equally impressive in truly artistic presentations.
Salem, near Llandeilo SA19 7LY
T: 01558 823394
E: eat@angelsalem.co.uk
www.angelsalem.co.uk

Bartrams at 698, Mumbles

The small façade hides the elegant contemporary style restaurant set in a sea front cottage. The open kitchen is very much in touch with culinary fashion. The novel use of local ingredients comes through in dishes such as seared scallops with laverbread linguini, tian of crab with tomato and avocado and chump of lamb with Nicoise tagliatelle. It serves breakfast, lunch, tea with patisserie and dinner.
698 Mumbles Road, Mumbles,
Swansea SA3 4EH
T: 01792 361616 E: info@698.uk.com
www.698.uk.com

Brazz, Stradey Park, Llanelli

Quality Welsh steaks and vegetarian food mark out this hotel in the town famous for its rugby team.
Stradey Park Hotel, Furnace, Llanelli SA15 4HA
T: 01554 758171 E: eat@the-brazz.com
www.the-brazz.com

Butchers Arms, Llanddarog

Hearty fare and generous portions mark this true Welsh country pub, with real ales and reasonable wines.
Llanddarog SA32 8NS
T: 01267 275330
www.butchersofllanddarog.co.uk

The Cawdor Arms, Llandeilo

This renowned town former coaching hotel has been totally refurbished by the same owners as Morgan's Swansea. Large rooms and suites all named after local castles have individual design and luxurious fittings and fabrics. The elegant restaurant has a young team cooking the fare of the county with enthusiasm.
Rhosmaen Street, Llandeilo SA19 6EN
T: 01558 823500
www.thecawdor.com

Cnapan, Newport

This pristine family run town house hotel has been a county institution for decades. Local fare cooked with elegant skill has kept in touch with contemporary culinary thinking. The varied menu shows understanding of ingredients and their use such as haddock fish cakes, seafood chowder, crab and smoked salmon tart, juicy lamb cutlets, laverbread sauces and wholemeal soda bread. Delightful comfortable bedrooms.
East Street, Newport SA42 0SY
T: 01239 820575 E: enquiry@cnapan.co.uk
www.cnapan.co.uk

Cors, Laugharne

Secluded in a superb garden this beautiful Victorian gentleman's country residence has an elegant faded glory and a wonderful laid back ambience. The cooking is sound using every local ingredient available. Lamb comes from the salt marshes of the heron-priested estuary and seafood includes sewin, bass, mullet, lobster, crab and mussels. Spacious basic bedrooms make for a relaxing stay.

The Cwtch restaurant at St David's has a relaxed atmosphere with friendly service.

Newbridge Road, Laugharne SA33 4SH
T: 01994 427219
www.the-cors.co.uk

Cwtch, St Davids

Very competent cooking and imaginative use of the most local of ingredients in a relaxed atmosphere with friendly service from an enthusiastic young team.
22 High Street, St Davids SA62 6SD
T: 01437 720491
E: info@cwtchrestaurant.co.uk
www.cwtchrestaurant.co.uk

Didier & Stephanie, Swansea

The pitch pine décor of this small restaurant is the setting for truly bourgeois French cuisine. Ingredients from Swansea Market are given the Gallic influence in dishes using perhaps cockles, laverbread, sewin and other Swansea-landed fish, or Gower salt marsh lamb, Welsh Black beef and game in season. The selection

of French wines and cheeses both show influence of the Bourgogne terroir.
56 St Helens Road, Swansea SA1 4BE
T: 01792 655603

Druidstone, Broad Haven

The imposing stone edifice perched on the cliff above St Brides bay has served homely cuisine for four decades. Its laid back no-frills approach takes one back to the original era. Hearty perhaps *avant-garde* food using Pembrokeshire produce is appreciated by the regular clientele and those who find this remote place. Real ales, reasonable wines, basic accommodation suit the amazing fresh Atlantic air.
Druidstone Haven, near Broad Haven, Haverfordwest SA62 3NE
T: 01437 781221
E: enquiries@druidstone.co.uk
www.druidstone.co.uk

Fairyhill, Reynoldston ●

This award-winning luxury restaurant with rooms on the beautiful Gower Peninsula has long been described as 'champion of local produce'. With its enthusiastic kitchen brigade it delivers some of the most interesting modern Welsh cuisine backed up by a fabulous wine cellar and well informed service. Gower lobster, crab, bass, salt marsh lamb, beef, and organic vegetables feature on the ever-creative seasonal menus.
Reynoldston, Gower SA3 1BS
T: 01792 390139
E: admin@fairyhill.net
www.fairyhill.net

Falcon, Carmarthen

Reliable home-cooked food in this convenient town centre hotel
Lammas Street, Carmarthen SA31 3AP
T: 01267 234959
E: reception@falconcarmarthen.co.uk
www.falconcarmarthen.co.uk

George's, Haverfordwest

A traditional pub serving real food. Steaks are first class on a sensibly varied menu.
24 Market Street, Haverfordwest SA61 1NH
T: 01437 766683

Hanson's at the Chelsea, Swansea

Sound confident cooking shows great personal flair and innovation. The range of fresh fish is always impressive and might include sewin, bass, sole, monk, hake and cod. Some meals are simply prepared; others in very modish style. Welsh Black beef and local lamb are treated with similar skill. This is the gem in a very cluttered area of the city centre.
17 St Mary's Street, Swansea SA1 3LH
T: 01792 464068

Hurrens Inn on the Estuary, Loughor

Smart modern bistro with daily fish specialities and prime Welsh meats that are very popular with locals.
13 Station Road, Loughor, Swansea SA4 6TR
T: 01792 899092

Hurst House, Laugharne

This is a wonderfully remote converted manor farmhouse. It has boutique bedrooms with all latest gadgets and designer fabrics; a new spa, swimming pool and cinema; and dining and drinking areas inside and out. They offer a range of food from simpler bar snacks to a full eclectic menu of modern European cooking from mainly locally sourced food including lamb from their own salt marsh.
East Marsh, Laugharne SA33 4RS
T: 01994 427417
www.hurst-house.co.uk

Jabajak, Whitland

This beautifully restored farmhouse serves inspired cuisine using local produce with herbs and vegetables from their own garden.
Banc y Llain, Llanboidy, Whitland, Carmarthenshire SA34 0ED
T: 01994 448786
E: info@jabajak.co.uk
www.jabajak.co.uk

King Arthur, Reynoldston

This truly fine pub with rooms is now an impressive catering operation. It has a locals' bar with fires and real ales, plus dining rooms and the largest function suite in the area. Local suppliers deliver daily an impressive range of fresh produce.
The basic dishes are the most successful where the fresh fish or meat speaks for itself.
Higher Green, Reynoldston, Gower SA3 1AD
T: 01792 390775
E: info@kingarthurhotel.co.uk
www.kingarthurhotel.co.uk

Knab Rock, Mumbles

New seafront boutique hotel overlooking Swansea bay serves French cuisine from local ingredients on an inspiring menu. Superb designer rooms.
734 Mumbles Road Mumbles SA3 4EL
T: 01792 361818
www.knabrock.com

La Braseria, Swansea

This large eating emporium serves great steaks and fresh fish best simply grilled on 'la parilla'. Great Spanish wines.
28 Wind Street, Swansea SA1 1DZ
T: 01792 469683
E: info@labraseria.com
www.labraseria.com

La Parilla, Swansea

An offshoot of the renowned La Braseria this spacious modern restaurant has similar food with grilled meat and fish and a wonderful wine cellar.
Kings Road, Swansea SA1 8PL
T: 01792 464530

Lamphey Court, Pembroke

Luxury hotel, spa and leisure complex.
Lamphey, Pembroke SA71 5NT
T: 01646 672273
E: info@lampheycourt.co.uk
www.lampheycourt.co.uk

Langlands Brasserie, Mumbles

Langlands Brasserie has the most superb setting in Gower – the tide ebbs and flows and surfers ride the great Atlantic breakers. The menu draws from the wonderful seafood and meat and produce from the Gower Peninsula. Meals open for breakfast, lunch, tea and dinner.
Brynfield Road, Swansea SA3 4SQ
T: 01792 363699
E: info@langlandsbrasserie.co.uk
www.langlandsbrasserie.co.uk

Lawtons at No 16, St Davids

Imaginative chef patron cooking of quality is making its mark in the city
16 Nun Street, St Davids SA62 6NS
T: 01437 729220
E: lawtonsatno16@aol.com
www.lawtonsatno16.com

Llys Meddyg, Newport

This beautifully furbished country house hotel has fine cuisine cooked by the proprietor. He buys as much local produce in season as possible and changes the menu regularly to keep his hotel guests and locals delighted.
East Street, Newport, Pembrokeshire SA42 0SY
T: 01239 820008
E: contact@llysmeddyg.com
www.llysmeddyg.com

Lower Haythog Farm, Spittal

Traditional country farmhouse cooking at its best in a renowned farm guesthouse.
Spittal, Haverfordwest SA62 5QL
T: 01437 731279
E: nesta@lowerhaythogfarm.co.uk
www.lowerhaythogfarm.co.uk

Maes yr Haf, Parkmill

This new restaurant with rooms in Gower has been decorated to very contemporary style and has a most competent kitchen. A high level of culinary skill comes across in both seafood and meat dishes. There are modern twists of style and novel use of fine ingredients many of which sourced very locally backed up with grand cuisine additions.
Parkmill, Gower SA3 2EH
T: 01792 371000
E: enquiries@maes-yr-haf.com
www.maes-yr-haf.com

Mermaid, Mumbles

This large restaurant has a reputation for good value and adventurous cooking. Its dedication to local ingredients is admirable.
686 Mumbles Road, Mumbles, Swansea SA3 4EE
T: 01792 367744

Morgan's, St Davids

This small town house restaurant has quality home-cooked food with a special emphasis on the locally landed seafood.
20 Nun Street, St Davids SA62 6NT
T: 01437 720508
E: eat@morgans-restaurant.co.uk
www.morgans-in-stdavids.co.uk

Morgans, Swansea

This beautifully restored building, formerly the offices of the Swansea Harbour Trust, is now one of the finest boutique hotels in the country. Spacious rooms, lounges, bars and restaurant are all tastefully designed and decorated in contemporary style. Lunch and dinner menus feature much

produce from Swansea Market and the local area.
Adelaide Street, Swansea SA1 1RR
T: 0800 988 3001
E: reception@morganshotel.co.uk
www.morganshotel.co.uk

No 13, Swansea

This smart modern restaurant serves generous home-cooked dishes.
13 Dillwyn Street, Swansea SA1 4AQ
T: 01792 522950

Norton House, Swansea

Modernised Georgian house has contemporary new bedrooms and sound traditional cooking.
Norton Road, Mumbles, Swansea SA3 5TQ
T: 01792 404891
E: enquiries@nortonhousehotel.co.uk
www.nortonhousehotel.co.uk

Old Kings Arms, Pembroke

This traditional town hostelry has been renowned for its fine table for decades. Direct contact with fishermen, farmers and foragers ensure the freshest fare of the county comes on inspired menus in the George Wheeler Restaurant and bars. Expect quality Welsh Black beef, local lamb, Dover sole, bass, lobster, crab, mussels and game in season.
Comfortable accommodation.
13 Main Street, Pembroke, SA71 4JS
T: 01646 683611
E: info@oldkingsarmshotel.co.uk
www.oldkingsarmshotel.co.uk

Old Pharmacy, Solva

Very close to where the local lobster boats land, this family-run restaurant offers a bounty from the sea. There is a variety of basic and eclectic dishes, using lobster, crab, mussels, bass, sewin, monkfish and whatever is landed in season. Local lamb and beef and well made modern and traditional puddings make for relaxed enjoyable dining.

5 Main Street, Solva, Pembrokeshire SA62 6UU
T: 01437 720005
www.theoldpharmacy.co.uk

Old Point House, Angle

This western whitewashed cottage pub has its own trawler. Expect wonderful fresh fish in the nautical bar and homely dining room. A must for fish lovers.
Angle Village, Angle, Pembroke SA71 5AS
T: 01646 641205

The Old Sailors, Pwllgwaelod

Close to the coast, and now with a stylish extension. Expect good things from the sea. Pwllgwaelod, Dinas Cross, Newport, Pembrokeshire SA42 0SE
T: 01348 811491

Patricks with Rooms, Mumbles

Popular restaurant with avant garde food in modern presentations.
Comfortable colonial style rooms.
638 Mumbles Road, Mumbles, Swansea SA3 4EA
T: 01792 360199
E: reception@patrickswithrooms.com
www.patrickswithrooms.com

Penally Abbey, Tenby

Traditional comforts of a country house hotel.
Penally, Pembrokeshire SA70 7PY
T: 01834 843033
E: info@penally-abbey.com
www.penally-abbey.com

Plough, Rhosmaen

Rebuilt, extended and modernised. The menu has 'old favourites' plus local items such as sewin, cockles and laverbread, and Edwinsford pheasant.
Rhosmaen, Llandeilo, Carmarthenshire SA19 6NP
T: 01558 823431
E: info@ploughrhosmaen.com
www.ploughrhosmaen.com

Something's Cooking, Letterston

Great fish and chip restaurant with many homemade specials.
The Square, Letterston, Pembrokeshire
SA62 5SB
T: 01348840621
www.somethingcooking.co.uk

St Brides Hotel, Saundersfoot

This hotel overlooks the sylvan cliffs and sandy bay of Saundersfoot. Totally refurbished with minimalist modern design to capture the views it has an art gallery, striking bar, elegant restaurant, amazing spa with infinite pool and superb bedrooms. The menu sings of the best fare of the county from land and sea and comes in contemporary presentations with style and flair.
St Brides Hill, Saundersfoot SA69 9NH
T: 01834 812304
E: reservations@stbridesspahotel.com
www.stbridesspahotel.com

Stable Door, Laugharne

This great cottage bistro is renowned for honest home cooking and good value.
Market Lane, Laugharne, Carmarthen, SA33 4SB
T: 01994 427777
E: wendy@stabledoor-restaurant-laugharne.com
www.laugharne-restaurant.co.uk

Stackpole Inn, Stackpole

This large country pub serves a range of bar and full meals.
Jasons Corner, Stackpole, Pembrokeshire
SA71 5DF
T: 01646 672324
E: info@stackpoleinn.co.uk
www.stackpoleinn.co.uk

Stone Hall, Welsh Hook

The French proprietor puts Gallic charm into this small hotel. The well presented local food comes on a short seasonally

Porthgain
– a former granite quarry village – the sheltered harbour is now a safe mooring for fishing boats. The Shed, was a net store, now a seafood bistro that has the pick of the catch.

● True Taste
Award winners

Refectory at St Davids

Dine in the cathedral itself for a surprisingly good experience from a well organised team.
St Davids Cathedral, St Davids, Pembrokeshire SA62 6RH
T: 01437 721760
E: info@refectoryatstdavids.co.uk
www.refectoryatstdavids.co.uk

The Shed, Porthgain ●

This is a must-do destination for all seafood lovers. The old granite quarries are silent, but fishing boats berth in the sheltered harbour. Freshest lobster and crab and other fish is landed daily.
This eaten as close to the sea as possible it has to be a joy in the old net store, now tea room bistro that overlooks the fish jetty.
Porthgain, Pembrokeshire SA62 5BN
T: 01348 831518
E: caroline@theshedporthgain.co.uk
www.theshedporthgain.co.uk

changing menu.
Stone Hall Mansion, Welsh Hook,
Haverfordwest SA62 5NS
T: 01348 840212
E: m.watson5@btconnect.com
www.stonehall-mansion.co.uk

Tides, Castlemorris

Neat modern bistro on a former cheese
farm specialises in fish from Cardigan Bay
and wonderful local meat.
Llangloffan Farm, Castlemorris SA62 5ET
T: 01348 891311

Two Cann Café, Swansea

A modern café wine bar serving all day food
in a great ambience.
Unit 2, J-Shed, Kings Road, Swansea
SA1 8PL
T: 01792 458000
E: info@cafetwocann.com
www.cafetwocann.com

Ty Mawr, Brechfa

Small country house hotel well known for
dinner parties.
Brechfa, Carmarthenshire SA32 7RA
T: 01267 202332

Valans, Llandybie

True neighbourhood restaurant with
enjoyable adventurous cooking.
29 High Street, Llandybie, Ammanford
SA18 3HX
T: 01269 851288
E: enquiries@valans.co.uk

Warpool Court, St Davids

This large Victorian mansion has splendid
grounds and an elegant dining room with
imaginative country house cuisine.
Warpool Court Hotel, St Davids SA62 6BN
T: 01437 720300
E: info@warpoolcourthotel.com
www.warpoolcourthotel.com

Welcome To Town Inn, Llanrhidian

This former country pub now a homely
restaurant is renowned for its skillful use
of Gower ingredients. Lamb comes from
the salt marshes of Llanrhidian close to
the coast, and now with a stylish extension,
expect good things, cockles from the sands
beyond. Lobster is from the rugged south
Gower coast along with bass, mackerel and
other fish. Cooking is accurate and flavours
well balanced.
Llanrhidian, Gower SA3 1EH
T: 01792 390015
www.thewelcometotown.co.uk

Wolfscastle Hotel

This renowned stone built country house hotel
has long been well known for its home style
cooking from prime produce of the county.
Wolfscastle, near Haverfordwest SA62 5LZ
T: 01437 741688
E: enquiries@wolfscastle.com
www.wolfscastle.com

Y Polyn, Nantgaredig

This modernised country pub has an
experienced team in the kitchen who know
the area and its food. Cooking is confident
with skilled precision at each level.
Capel Dewi, Nantgaredig SA32 7LH
T: 01267 290000

Yr Hen Dafarn, Llansteffan

This little former pub operates as a
restaurant for bookings only. Expect
the freshest home caught fish, garden
vegetables and proprietor-shot game.
A short menu might have flounder, sewin,
bass, crayfish, crab, hare, woodcock and
pheasant according to season. The food
has real gusto cooked with confidence
and delivering true flavour. Portions are
generous and wine reasonably priced.
Llansteffan SA33 5JY
T: 01267 241656

South West Wales: where to buy and producers

Freshly harvested Savoy cabbage.

Taste of the County stocks an array of local and Welsh produce and is considered one of the most successful farm shops in the area.

Laverbread is a traditional Welsh ingredient. Made into laverballs it can be served as a starter or with a main meal on menus throughout Wales.

Rich in produce

The prosperous South West Wales has rich farmland – in Pembroke, Carmarthenshire and Gower – plus the wonderful unspoilt coastline with beautiful beaches. There are many busy towns including Haverfordwest, Carmarthen, Llanelli, Llandeilo and Llandovery and the vibrant City of Swansea. The area not only produces a vast amount and variety of food, but has the population as an eager market at all levels.

Food festivals

Fish has always been important to the economy of the area from the pre-war days when great fleets of deep-sea trawlers operated from Milford Haven and Swansea. The present inshore fleets operating from many of the harbours and tiny sheltered bays land a wide variety of fish and shellfish. This is celebrated every year at the Pembrokeshire Fish Festival in June. The week long event covers many aspects of fishing and associated business and leisure activities. Cooking demonstrations, parties, barbecues and special menus in all local restaurants add to the fun of the week.

Carmarthen with its rich agricultural meat and dairy industries holds several produce markets throughout the year, particularly at Christmas and St David's Day. Small yet popular festivals are held at Llandeilo. Expect to see many of the quality Welsh farmhouse cheese producers such as Nantybwla, Llanboidy, Teifi Farmhouse, Carmarthenshire Cheese Company and Cothi Valley Goats, plus many quality farm meats and vegetables.

Farmers' markets

Farmers' markets are held regularly across the area. The most notable is the fortnightly Haverfordwest farmers' market held on the banks of the Western Cleddau in the town. All produce has to be from a 40 mile radius and every market attracts a wide range of food companies and an enthusiastic public. Organic meat, poultry, fish and shellfish, farmed trout, vegetables and dairy produce of the very best are at truly rural prices.

Farmers' and local produce markets have proliferated in the last decade held regularly at Mumbles, Penclawdd and Llangennith in Gower, Llandovery, Fishguard, Pembroke and Carmarthen.

Swansea Market

The original farmers' market could be said to be Swansea Market where alongside the permanent stalls are rows of tables where local farmers from Gower can rent space on a daily basis. The vegetable farmers of Rhossili have a regular fine display of produce from their farms that are still cultivated to the ancient strip farming system. Friday and Saturday sees every table groaning with vegetables, eggs, bread, cheese and poultry, plus flowers and garden plants.

In the past the cockle and laverbread producers from Penclawdd used these tables, but they are now in a central area with purpose built refrigeration units. Many people still visit the market and eat a bag of fresh cockles as they do their shopping, then pick up a Welsh cake hot from the griddle. Under the one roof there are several butchers, many fruit and vegetable stalls, bakers, cooked meat companies with their own Welsh cured bacon, sausages, faggots, butter, ham, pork pies, pasties and eggs. Three excellent fishmongers will have, in season, much locally landed and line-caught fish. The iced counters will have Swansea Bay plaice, dabs, flounders, sole, brill, turbot, monkfish and skate. In season, sewin and salmon, crab and lobster, scallops, oysters and samphire make a most colourful local showcase. Visit Coakley Green, Tuckers and Dragon Fish. Gower meat at its best can be found at Huw Phillips's stall in the market, all from his own farm and abattoir at Llanmorlais. Welsh Black beef, lamb and pork are exceptional. Also visit Vaughan's, Upton's and the other butchers around the periphery of the market.

Dewi Roberts in Llandeilo sources meat for his shop from farms he personally knows across South Wales. He home-produces all cooked meats and pies.

Carmarthen Market

Carmarthen Market has a splendid selection similar to Swansea but with a few local additions. Carmarthen ham from Albert Rees was the first dry-cured ham produced in Britain, made to an old family recipe that dates back generations. Alongside this they sell other Welsh charcuterie including sausages, faggots and bacon. Sewin as fresh as it comes from the Tywi Estuary might come from the coracle fishermen of Carmarthen and the boats of Ferryside. Deep emerald green samphire gathered by hand from the salt marshes of Laugharne makes a colourful contrast to the glistening fish on Raymond Rees's fish slab. Alongside there will be salt marsh lamb from Laugharne and Welsh Black beef on Dai Rees the butcher's counter. Local vegetables, Welsh farmhouse cheeses, home-baked bread, bara brith and Welsh cakes make shopping in this market a delight.

Butchers and delis

Independent food shops, delicatessens and butchers who make the effort to stock and display local food are thriving. Eynons of St Clears is another example of an independent butcher that has developed into a superb food hall. The selection of fresh meat has the expected salt marsh lamb, Welsh Black beef, free-range poultry, pork and game. It comes skilfully butchered or made into a wide selection of cooked dishes alongside which is a comprehensive selection of pantry and luxury produce.

Welsh Black beef is the focus at Cig Calon Cymru in Cross Hands, a state-of-the-art butcher linked to their own abattoir and farms. Dewi Roberts of Fairfach Llandeilo knows all the local farmers who supply his premium range that draws customers from a wide area, and the hundreds who order from him on the internet. Wollacotts of Newton in Mumbles have wonderful beef from their own farm, lamb and pork from other family members in Gower and West Wales. Home-cooked food includes fine bacon, sausages, ham, faggots and pies, plus they have a good selection of vegetables, cheese and preserves. Hughes of Fishguard is renowned for his sausages that include seafood varieties, and for his prime Welsh meat and selection of freshly landed fish from local boats. Howells of Penclawdd can survey the lambs grazing on the salt marshes opposite the shop that also has fine local Welsh Beef, lamb and free-range meats.

Many farms are now selling their produce from their farm gate or farm shops. Others might sell as an extension of a wholesale depot. Welsh Quality Meats of Neyland, Welsh Hook Meat Centre near Haverfordwest, Bethesda Fresh Farm Meats, Cig Lodor Preseli and Cambrian Organics of Llandysul are among some of the excellent suppliers of the area.

Fruit and vegetables

Farm shops and pick-your-own are plentiful in Gower, Carmarthenshire and Pembrokeshire. Many open just for the season so look out for signs in hedges and on farm gates. These can often offer the best value for money if you are happy to trudge the fields. In Gower look for Beynon's Nicholston Farm and PYO. In Pembroke Priory Farm Shop, Tenby, Springfields shop and PYO, Spring Meadow near St David's, and Yerbeston Gate Farm near Carew all have a home grown selection. The Farm Shop at Taste of the County, Bethesda Cross, Saundersfoot is recognised as one of the most successful in the area.

Seafood

This is a great area for buying fine produce from the sea. As well as the markets a large number of fish suppliers and cottage industries utilise that which is not shipped to the continent. Crab processing has increased on both a cottage scale and in some purpose built units such as Dash Shellfish of Little Haven, Claws Shellfish of Pembroke, Neville George of Croesgoch, and Colin Brown of Neyland. Tenby Seafare, Newport Fish and Coakley in Mumbles all have reputations for best fresh fish of the area.

Delicatessens

The range of produce from this area gives chefs, home cooks and retailers an amazing selection of food as the seasons unfold through the year. It can keep markets and menus packed with local ingredients that have a very low carbon footprint with only local food miles.

Independent delicatessens, such as the Narberth branch of Ultracomida, have a wide range of cheese and specialist produce.

A full spectrum of Welsh produce, especially the fare of the west, can be found particularly the fare of the west can be found at Castell Howell Foods in Carmarthen. As the largest wholesaler of Welsh produce with distribution throughout Wales they also have a cash-and-carry with a full range of fresh and frozen produce, larder goods and ready meals.

● True Taste
Award winners

markets, shops, specialists and producers in South West Wales

A & G Williams Felinfoel Faggots
Traditional Welsh savoury products.
24 Park View, Felinfoel, Llanelli SA14 8BH
T: 01554 757751

A J Rees and Sons
Traditional butcher and local wholesaler.
29 High Street, Narberth SA67 7AR
T: 01834 861892

Abertrinant Free Range Eggs
True free-range hens – fresh quality eggs.
Abertrinant, Blaenffos, Boncath SA37 0HX
T: 01239 841321

Albert Rees
Dry-cured and traditional, ham, sausages, faggots and cooked meats.
15 Market Precinct, Carmarthen SA31 1QY
T: 01267 231204
www.carmarthenham.co.uk

Barita Delicatessen
Modern traditional delicatessen with Welsh foods.
139a Rhosmaen Street, Llandeilo SA19 6EN
T: 01558 823444
E: rita@barita.co.uk
www.barita.co.uk

Beacons Smoked
Smoked fish and meats.
Pant-Y-Cefn, Gwynfe, Llangadog SA19 9RF
T: 01550 740360

Bethesda Butter
Green pastures produce sweetest milk that makes the most sublime dairy produce.
Sarngwm, Bethesda, Narberth SA67 8HG
T: 01437 563039
E: llaethbethesda@tiscali.co.uk

Bethesda Fresh Farm Meats
Own farm-produced fresh meats and cured produce.
Rose Villa, Bethesda, Narberth SA67 8HQ
T: 01437 563124
E: sales@bffm.co.uk
www.fresh-welsh-meat.co.uk

Beynon's Nicholaston Farm
PYO strawberries, raspberries, gooseberries, redcurrants. Also has a farm shop restocked daily with fresh local produce.
Penmaen, Gower, SA3 2HL
T: 01792 371209
www.nicholastonfarm.co.uk

Brecon Beacons Natural Waters Brecon Carreg
Natural spring water, still and sparkling.
Llwyndewi Isaf, Trap, Llandeilo SA19 6TT
T: 01269 850175
E: sales@spa.co.uk
www.breconwater.co.uk

Bumpylane Organics
Rare-breed organic beef and lamb, and speciality sausages and puddings.
Shortlands Farm, Druidston, Haverfordwest SA62 3NE
T: 01437 781234
E: info@bumpylane.co.uk
www.bumpylane.co.uk

Caeremlyn Turkeys
Traditional free-range turkeys.
Caeremlyn, Henllan, Amgoed, Whitland SA34 0SJ
T: 01994 240260
E: enquiries@caeremlyn.co.uk
www.caeremlyn.co.uk

Caerfai Farm Cheeses
Farm-produced organic cheddar and farm shop.
Caerfai, St Davids SA62 6QT
T: 01437 720548
www.cawscheese.co.uk

Caws Cenarth Cheese produces award-winning cheeses including the speciality flavoured Cennin Cenarth, Brady Braf and Tomi Twyn.

Calon Wen Organic Foods ●

Organic dairy produce from organic co-operative.
Unit 4, Whitland Industrial Estate, Whitland SA34 0HR
T: 01994 241368
www.calonwen.co.uk

Cambrian Organics

Locally sourced organic meat from nominated farms.
Horeb, Llandysul SA44 4JG
T: 01559 363151
E: info@cambrianorganics.com
www.cambrianorganics.com

Carmarthen Ham

Dry-cured ham producers, and traditional Welsh hams and cured meats.
Arfryn, Uplands, Carmarthen SA32 8DX
T: 01267 237687
E:info@carmarthenham.co.uk
www.carmarthenham.co.uk

Carmarthen Market

Town market with traditional producers and retailers.
St Catherine Street, Carmarthen SA31 1QY
T: 01267 228841
www.carmarthenmarket.co.uk

Carmarthenshire Cheese Company Pont Gâr

Range of cheeses includes brie style, Llangloffan cheddar and goats' cheese.
Boksburg Hall, Llanllwch, near Carmarthen SA31 3RN
T: 01267 221168
E: sales@carmarthenshirechesse.co.uk
www.carmarthenshirecheese.co.uk

Castell Howell Foods

Largest wholesaler and distributor of Welsh food produce, and cash and carry.
Cross Hands Food Park, Cross Hands SA14 6SX
T: 01269 846080 E: enquiries@chfoods.co.uk
www.castellhowellfoods.co.uk

Caws Cenarth Cheese ●

Traditional organic cheeses include Caerphilly, brie style and blue.
Glyneithinog, Pontseli, Boncath SA37 0LH
T: 01239 710432
E: cenarth.cheese@virgin.net
www.cawscenarth.co.uk

Celtic Pride

Quality produced beef from nominated farms.
Llysonnen Mill, Travellers Rest, Carmarthen SA31 3SG
T: 01267 222919
www.welshmeat.net

Cig Calon Cymru

Specialists in Welsh Black beef and local lamb.
Clos Gelliwerdd, Cross Hands Business Park, Cross Hands SA14 6RE
T: 01269 844471
E: info.cigcaloncymru@virgin.net
www.cigcaloncymru.co.uk

● True Taste
Award winners

Cig Lodor Preseli Lamb
Lamb specialists in Preseli mountains.
Lodor Fach, Maenclochog, Clunderwen
SA66 7RD
T: 01437 532277

Claws Shellfish ●
Seafood producers and processors, notable
for crab.
Lodge Gate, Hazel Hill, Llanstadwell,
Milford Haven SA73 1EZ
T: 01646 601010
E: clawsshellfish@tiscali.co.uk

Clover Jerseys
Jersey herd cream and butter.
Cwrcoed Farm, Llangoedmor SA43 2LG
T: 01239 621658

Coakley Green
Specialist fishmonger with local and
national suppliers.
41c Swansea Market, Oxford Street,
Swansea SA1 3PF
T: 01792 653416

Coakley of Mumbles
Specialist fishmonger with local and
national suppliers.
5 Newtown Road, Mumbles, Swansea
SA3 4AR
T: 01792 368075

Cothi Valley Goats
Own herd goats' cheese in many styles
– soft, hard and creamy.
Cilwr Farm, Talley, Llandeilo SA19 7BQ
T: 01558 685555
E: goat@homested.fsbusiness.co.uk
www.cothivalleygoats.co.uk

Cwm Deri Vineyard
Vineyard, country wines and shop.
Martletwy, Narberth SA67 8AP
T: 0 1834 891274
E: enquiries@cwm-deri.co.uk
www.cwm-deri.co.uk

Dash Shellfish ●
Shellfish processors noted for crab.
Little Haven SA62 3UA
T: 07917 353323
www.dashshellfish.co.uk

Dewi Roberts Butchers
Local butcher specialising in traceability
of produce.
16 Tywi Terrace, Ffairfach, Llandeilo
SA19 6ST
T: 01558 822566

Dragon Fish
Traditional fishmongers with a well
presented counter.
57b Swansea Market, Swansea SA1 3PQ
T: 01792 655664

Drim Farm Foods
Clotted cream from own Jersey herd.
Drim Farm, Llawhaden, Narberth SA67 8DN
T: 01437 541295

Einon Valley Lamb
Local farm lamb.
Gaerwen, Uchaf Rhos, Llandysul SA44 5AH
T: 01559 370884
E: einonvalley@hotmail.com

Evan-Evans Brewery ●
Traditional cask conditioned and
bottled ales.
The New Brewery, 1 Rhosmaen Street,
Llandeilo SA19 6LU
T: 01588 824455
www.evan-evans.com

Eynon's of St Clears
Quality butcher and food hall with many
local meats, game and cooked meals.
Deganwy, Pentre Road, St Clears SA33 4LR
T: 0800 7315816
E: enquiries@eynons.co.uk
www.eynons.co.uk

Run by the Curtis family, Dash supply brown crab and lobster live, cooked or processed.

Felinfoel Brewery Company

Traditional brewery noted for cask ales and bottled beers.
Farmers Row, Felinfoel, Llanelli SA14 8LB
T: 01554 773357
E: enquires@felinfoel-brewery.com
www.felinfoel-brewery.com

Ferm Tyllwyd Organic Black Beef

Farm-reared Welsh Black beef specialist.
Felingwm-Uchaf, Carmarthen SA32 7QE
T: 01267 290537
E: johntyllwyd@hotmail.com
www.organicwelshblackbeef.co.uk

Ffynnon Organics

Vegetables and fruit in box schemes locally.
Ffynnon Samson, Llangloman, Clynderwen SA66 7QL
T: 01437 532542 E: info@enjoypreseli.co.uk
www.enjoypreseli.co.uk

Fiona's Fudge

Homemade rich fruit cakes and fudge.
Coed Y Ceirw, Broad Oak, Carmarthen SA32 8QS
T: 07977 097957
E: fionas.fudge@dsl.pipex.com

Fish Plaice Walter Davies & Sons

Fish merchant and shop with some locally landed fish.
The Docks, Milford Haven SA37 3AE
T: 01646 692331

Goodies

Delicatessen and cheese shop.
57A Swansea Market, Oxford Street, Swansea SA1 3PQ
T: 07793 589596
E: goodies-cheese@ntlworld.com

● True Taste
Award winners

Gower Coast Seafoods

Cockle and laverbread harvester and producer.
72 Pencaerfenni Lane, Crofty, Penclawdd, Swansea SA4 3SW
T: 01792 850796

Gwaun Valley Meats ●

Own cured bacon and gammon specialist.
Pontfaen, Fishguard SA65 9SD
T: 01348 881295
E: gwaun@btinternet.com

Harmony Herd ●

Specialist rare-breed pork, sausages and cured products.
Bowls Farm, Beulah, Newcastle Emlyn SA38 9QU
T: 01239 810740
www.harmonyherd.co.uk

Heavenly

Artistic chocolates and homemade ice cream with many flavours.
Rhosmaen Street, Llandeilo SA19 6EN
T: 01558 822800
E: shop@heavenlychoc.co.uk
www.heavenlychoc.co.uk

Hillside Smokery

Traditionally smoked fish and meat.
Unit 1, Old Station Yard, Crymych SA41 3RL
T: 01239 831515
E: hillsidesmokery@tiscali.co.uk
www.hillsidesmokery.co.uk

Howells of Penclawdd

Quality butcher with local suppliers of salt marsh lamb and Welsh Black beef.
11 Cae Folland, Penclawdd, Swansea
T: 01792 850371

Pencae Mawr produce a range of organic traditional chutneys and jellies available to buy in selected farm shops and delicatessens.

Heavenly ice cream from freshest dairy milk and natural flavours.

Hughes Butcher & Fresh Fish
Butcher and fishmonger noted for innovative meat and seafood sausages.
Anchor House, 4 High Street, Fishguard SA65 9AR
T: 01348 872394

Hurns Brewing Company ●
Specialist in traditional Welsh ales.
Unit 3 Century Park, Swansea Enterprise Park, Swansea SA6 8RP
T: 01792 797300
E: beer@hurns.co.uk
www.hurnsbeer.co.uk

Huw Phillips
Own farm Gower meat noted for spring lamb and Welsh Black beef.
55c Swansea Market, Oxford Street, Swansea SA1 3PF
T: 01792 455100

Jenkins Butchers and Ty Croeso Delicatessen
Butchers shop with all homemade produce, and modern delicatessen next door.
Angel Shop, Market Square, Newcastle Emlyn SA38 9AQ
T: 01239 710343

Kid Me Not
Goats' milk products include flavoured fudge and cheeses.
Ffynnongrech Farm, Talley, Llandeilo SA19 7BZ
T: 01558 685935
E: info@kidmenot.co.uk
www.kidmenot.co.uk

Kite Wholefoods
Organic mayonnaise from free-range eggs.
Y Cadw, 38 Ffordd Aneurin, Pontyberem SA15 5DF
T: 01269 871035
E: enquiries@kitewholefoods.co.uk
www.kitewholefoods.co.uk

Leslie A Parsons & Sons (Burry Port) ●
Bottled cockles, mussels, pickles and laverbread.
Ashburnham Works, Burry Port SA16 0ET
T: 01554 833351
E: sales@parsonspickles.co.uk
www.parsonspickles.co.uk

Llanboidy Cheesemakers ●
Traditional farmhouse cheddar and organic cheese.
Cilowen Uchaf Farm, Whitland SA34 0TJ
T: 01994 448303
E: sue@llanboidycheese.co.uk
www.llanboidycheese.co.uk

Miranda's Preserves
Wide range of artisan-produced pickles, preserves and chutneys.
Ty'r Henner, Goodwick, Pembrokeshire SA64 0JB
T: 01348 872011
E: mirandajam@btinternet.com
www.mirandas-preserves.co.uk

Nantybwla Farmhouse Cheese
Traditional cheese from own farm milk includes cheddar and Caerphilly.
Nantybwla Farm, College Road, Carmarthen SA31 3QS
T: 01267 237905

Neath Indoor Market
Town market with traditional producers and retailers.
Green Street, Neath SA11 1DP

Organic Pantry
Organic vegetables and other produce from shop or delivered.
Margaret Street, Ammanford SA18 3AB
T: 01269 596931
www.organics-online.co.uk

Organics to Go

Box scheme of meat, vegetables, salad and dairy produce throughout South Wales.
Werndolau Farm, Gelli Aur,
Carmarthen SA32 8NE
T: 01558 668088
E: enquiries@organicstogo.info
www.organicstogo.info

Pant Mawr

Artisan cheese from cows' and goats' milk; soft and traditional styles.
Pant Mawr Farm, Rosebush, Clunderwen,
SA66 7QU
T: 01437 532627
E: pantmawrJennings@hotmail.com
www.pantmawrcheeses.co.uk

Pembertons Victorian Chocolates

Handmade artistic chocolates.
The Welsh Chocolate Farm, Llanboidy
SA34 0EX
T: 01994 448800
www.welshchocolatefarm.com

Pembrokeshire Coast Organic Meats

Farm-assured organic beef and lamb with traceability.
Cwmrath Farm, Stepaside, Narberth
SA67 8LU
T: 01834 813239
E: info@pembrokeshirecoastorganicmeat.co.uk
www.pembrokeshirecoastorganicmeats.co.uk

Pembrokeshire Fish Farms

Farmed trout for sport and the table.
Orielton Mill, Hundleton, Pembroke
SA71 5QT
T: 01646 661393

Pembrokeshire Pork and Sausages

Ethically produced pork, lamb and beef to highest standards.

Friesian cows on lush pasture produce superb milk for Trioni.

Dolwerdd Farm, Boncath SA37 0JW
T: 01239 841268
E: info@pembrokeshirepork.co.uk
www.pembrokeshirepork.co.uk

Pencae Mawr Farm Foods ●
Organic preserves, chutneys and condiments.
Pencae Mawr Farm, Llanfynydd SA32 7TR
T: 01558 668613

Pen-lon Cottage Brewery ●
Artisan ales of individual character.
Penlon Farm, Pencae, Llanarth SA47 0QN
T: 01545 580022 E: beer@penlon.biz
www.penlon.biz

Pommes
Catering specialist for private and corporate events.
Felindre House, Felindre, Llandysul SA44 5XG
T: 01559 370318
E: enquiries@pommes.co.uk
www.pommes.co.uk

Popty Cara
Bara brith, Welsh cakes, fruit cakes and puddings.
Home Farm, Lawrenny, Kilgetty SA68 0PN
T: 01646 651690 E: enquiries@poptycara.co.uk
www.poptycara.co.uk

Prime Beef Company
Quality well hung beef.
Ffynonau. Henllan Amgoed, Whitland SA34 0SG
T: 01994 241050

Prince's Gate
Bottled natural spring water – still and sparkling.
New House Farm, Prince's Gate, Narbeth SA67 8JD
T: 01834 831225
E: info@princesgatespringwater.com
www.princesgatespringwater.com

Priory Farm Shop
Farm-produced fruit and vegetables and PYO.
Priory Farm, New Hedges, Tenby SA70 8TN
T: 01834 844662

Puffin Produce
Pembrokeshire potato specialist.
Withybush, Haverfordwest SA62 4BS
T: 01437 766716

Raymond Rees
Top-quality sewin and other fish from local boats in season.
Carmarthen Market, Carmarthen SA31 1QY
T: 01267 234144

S & J Organics – Welsh Organic Poultry
Welsh chickens, geese, turkeys and guinea fowl. Farm gate sales.
Llwyncrychyddod, Llanpumsaint, Carmarthen SA33 6JS
T: 01267 253570 E: info@sjorganics.co.uk
www.sjorganics.co.uk

Sanclêr Organic Yoghurt Cheese
Natural organic milk yogurt cream cheese, plus flavoured versions.
Glancynin, St Clears SA33 4JR
T: 01994 232999
E: sanclerorganic@aol.com
www.sanclerorganic.co.uk

Saputo Cheese UK Ltd
Large producer of catering cheese.
The Creamery, Aberarad, Newcastle Emlyn SA38 9DQ
T: 01239 710424
www.saputo.com

True Taste
Award winners

Selwyn's Penclawdd Seafoods

Cockles and laverbread from Gower.
Lynch Factory, Marsh Road, Llanmorlais,
Swansea SA4 3TN
T: 01792 851945
E: selwynsseafoods@btconnect.com
www.selwynsseafoods.co.uk

Sir Benfro Bakery

Wide range of fresh bread and cakes.
Unit 9, Spring Gardens Industrial Estate,
Whitland SA34 0HZ
T: 01994 241177

Spring Meadow Farm Shop

Own farm-produced fresh vegetables.
Caerfarchell, St Davids SA62 6XG
T: 01437 721800

Springfields Farm Shop

Home grown asparagus, vegetables and
fruit, plus foraged produce.
Red House Hill, Manorbier,
Tenby SA70 7SL
T: 01834 871746

St Davids Food and Wine

Delicatessen, local foods and wine.
High Street, St Davids SA62 6SB
T: 01437 721948
E: info@stdavidsfoodandwine.co.uk
www.stdavidsfoodandwine.co.uk

Swansea Market

Largest covered market in Wales with
abundance of local produce.
Oxford Street, Swansea SA1 3PF
T: 01792 546545
E: info@food-passion.co.uk
www.swanseamarket.food-passion.co.uk

Taste of the County ●

Fresh fruit and vegetables, dairy produce to
pickles and preserves.
The Farm Shop, Bethesda Cross,
Saundersfoot SA69 9DS
T: 01834 812911

Tenby Sea Fayre

Fresh fish from county and beyond.
Old Market Hall, High Street, Tenby
SA70 7EU
T: 01834 844811

Tregroes Waffle Bakery

Sweet waffles to traditonal recipes.
Unit 2, Pencader Road, Llandysul SA44 4AE
T: 01559 363468
E: sales@tregroeswaffles.co.uk
www.tregroeswaffles.co.uk

Trioni ●

Flavoured dairy drinks.
Ffosyficer, Abercych, Boncath SA37 0EU
T: 01239 682572
www.trioni.com

Tucker's Fishmongers

Local and seasonal seafood with fresh fish
daily.
62/63 Swansea Market, Oxford Street,
Swansea SA1 3PQ
T: 01792 652277
www.tuckersseafood.food-passion.co.uk

Tŷ Nant Spring Water

Designer presented spring water –
still and sparkling.
Bethania, Llanon SY23 5LS
T: 01974 272111
E: info@tynant.com
www.tynant.com

Ultracomida Delicatessen ●

Traditional and modern style delicatessen
with abundant local foods.
7 High Street, Narberth SA67 7AR
T: 01834 861491

Vicars Mill Trout Farm

Quality farmed trout from clear brook
waters of Pembrokeshire.
Llandissilio, Pembrokeshire SA66 7LS
T: 01437 563553
E: info@vicarsmilltroutfarm.co.uk
www.welsh-trout.co.uk

South West Wales: where to buy and producers

Welsh Barrow
Artisan canned laverbread and canned cockles.
PO Box 218, Mumbles, Swansea SA3 4ZA
T: 020 7793 7085
www.laverbread.org.uk

Welsh Haven Products
Free-range organic poultry.
Millin View Farm, Lower Quay Road, Hook, Haverfordwest SA62 4LR
T: 01437 891433

Welsh Hook Meat Centre
Organic meat – Welsh lamb, Black beef, free-range pork. Retail shop.
Woodfield, Withybush Road, Haverfordwest SA62 4BW
T: 01437 768876
E: enquiries@welshhook.co.uk
www.welshhook.co.uk

The Welsh Mustard Company
Firey mustard and garden fresh mint sauce.
Maes Aeron, Ciliau Aeron
SA48 8BP
T: 01570 471497
E: info@welshmustard.com
www.welshmustard.com

Welsh Quality Meats
Top quality wholesale butchers for locally sourced meats.
Ty Sir Benfro House, Brunel Quay, Neyland SA73 1PY
T: 01646 601816
E: wqm@btconnect.com
www.welshqualitymeats.co.uk

Wendy Brandon Handmade Preserves
Jams, pickles, chutneys and preserves.
Felin Wen, Boncath, SA37 0JR
T: 01239 841568
E: wendy@wendybrandon.co.uk
www.wendybrandon.co.uk

Wholefoods of Newport
Wide selection of vegetables and wholefoods.
East Street, Newport, Pembrokeshire SA42 0SY
T: 01239 820773

Will & Jamie's Fresh Yoghurt Drinks
Fresh fruit flavoured yogurt drinks directly from milk from their own farm.
Keystone Hill Farm, Keystone, Haverfordwest SA62 6EJ
T: 07710 972963
www.willandjamies.co.uk

Woollacotts Butchers
Traditional butcher with own farm and locally sourced meat.
15 Nottage Road, Newton, Mumbles SA3 47U
T: 01792 366020

Yerbeston Gate Farm Shop ●
Welsh Black beef, lamb, saddleback pork, Welsh drinks, preserves.
Yerbeston, Kilgetty SA68 0NS
T: 01834 891637
E: info@farmshopfood.co.uk
www.farmshopfood.co.uk

south West Wales: where to buy and producers 107

south East Wales

The village of Pendoylan is surrounded by open farming country even though it is only a few miles from the Welsh capital.

South East Wales

South of the Beacons to the Bristol Channel is industrial Wales where regeneration reigns. The Welsh Valleys no longer have industrial blight but vibrant hi-tech businesses set in modern parks. Prosperity spreads from the capital Cardiff into the affluent Vale of Glamorgan and the land where Usk and Wye flow through Monmouthshire. The top restaurants and caterers soak up the produce brought the short way from the coast and pastures of Wales.

Monmouth

Abergavenny

Merthyr Tydfil

Raglan

Aberdare

Pontypridd

Chepstow

Llantrisant

Newport

Bridgend

Caerphilly

Pendoylan

Porthcawl

Cardiff

Cowbridge

Barry

South East Wales: about the area

Llanerch Vineyard stands in more than 20 acres of the Glamorgan countryside. Vines were first planted at Llanerch in 1986 with subsequent plantings each year up to 1991.

Cowbridge, a busy market town, now an affluent, bustling place of restaurants, wine bars and boutiques.

This is the most densely populated part of Wales, more urban than rural, containing several major towns, the city of Newport and the capital, Cardiff. Much of it is industrial landscape that shows the continual change that has taken place since the Industrial Revolution, with coal mining and iron and steel making the main features for two centuries. In the last two decades the industrial, business and administrative focus has changed dramatically.

The area is defined in the south by the coastline that runs from the Afan to the Wye estuaries with the fertile Vale of Glamorgan and the tidal Severn Estuary as its main features. The northern limit is approximately the Heads of the Valleys Road. Here the land south of the Brecon Beacons is known as the Welsh Valleys, noted for the coal and iron industry. The border county of Monmouthshire is the greener area with the Usk and Wye Valleys in a rolling rural landscape.

Cardiff

Cardiff is now one of the most vibrant cities in Britain. The former docks have been regenerated as the exciting business, leisure and residential area of Cardiff Bay. The historic buildings of Butetown have been joined by hi-tech businesses, exclusive apartments, the Wales Millennium Centre, the five-star St David's Hotel, restaurants, wine bars and the Senedd, home of the National Assembly for Wales.

The Cardiff Bay Barrage that caused a lot of controversy prior to construction has proved to be a great success creating a waterway that links as far up river as the Millennium Stadium. It forms the heart of the area and water taxis make communication with Penarth and the marina very easy.

The centre of Cardiff has remained the hub of the city. The Millennium Stadium has a continual programme of sporting events and entertainment. It puts Cardiff in a unique position as the only city in the world where the main stadium is at the centre of

the city, within easy reach of restaurants, hotels, bars, cafes and major shops.

Some of the 'must-sees' in the area are National Museum Cardiff, St Fagans National History Museum, Cardiff Bay with the fine Wales Millennium Centre for opera and other performing arts, and the splendid Millennium Stadium itself.

Cardiff has several modern shopping malls together with peripheral city shopping areas such as Culverhouse Cross. Yet alongside this are the famous arcades that link the main traditional streets of the city centre. These are the place to find the best coffee shops, cafés, delicatessens, designer clothes shops, wine bars and restaurants.

The city centre has several luxury hotels that cater for the business community and tourists, all within easy reach of the city's main attractions for business and social life and tourist destinations. Though catering in the city is well geared to the fast life surrounding the Millennium Stadium there are several restaurants of note with a more relaxed style of dining.

Vale of Glamorgan

The Vale is the area south of the coalfield where wealthy rural estates dominate the scene. There are numerous smaller picturesque villages and towns that have an air of affluence that has spread from Cardiff over the years. The former market town of Cowbridge is now one of the most exclusive places with designer shops, delicatessens, café bars and restaurants. Throughout the vale each village has its local hostelry many of which have been renowned for decades and still retain a traditional rural ambience.

Coast

The coastline of the Vale of Glamorgan is particularly beautiful consisting mainly of limestone rising vertically to 70 metres from the beaches. Delightful sandy beaches at Porthcawl, Southerndown and St Donats have large areas for summer relaxation. A famous landmark, Tusker Rock off Southerndown covers hundreds of acres at low tide and over the years has claimed many ships that have incorrectly navigated these treacherous waters.

The tidal range of the Bristol Channel and the mouth of the Severn is the second highest in the world after the Bay of Fundy in Canada. The range of up to 15 metres means that great areas of foreshore are exposed at low tide.

There have long been schemes for harnessing the natural force of the tide to generate power, the most ambitious of which is a barrage across the Severn Estuary. However a project of this magnitude seems some way off as yet.

The Wye Valley surrounds a 72-mile stretch of the meandering river Wye between Chepstow in Wales and Hereford in England.

Valleys

The land north of the M4 to the Heads of the Valleys road and east to the A4042 Pontypool to Abergavenny road is the main Welsh coal mining area known as the Welsh valleys. Shaped by the Ice Age the land of over 600 metres high is dissected by the rivers Rhondda, Taff and Rhymney flowing south-eastward to the Bristol Channel. These were the routes for coal to the main ports for exporting this valuable fuel in the last two centuries. With the regeneration of the land much has been planted with fir trees to conceal the industrial spoil, and some large areas have become green fields again with farming returning to the valleys. Many hi-tech companies have settled in Wales and it is now very different from a quarter of a century ago.

Industry

The County of Monmouthshire is undulating land of the Usk Valley extending to the Wye and Monnow Valleys and as far north as the Black Mountains, taking in the pretty Vale of Ewyas, the peaceful setting of Llanthony Abbey. The terrain is quite different from the coal-mining valleys with only a few small areas where industrial exploitation is evident. It is an area of large country estates

The tranquillity of the green valley at Llanthony Abbey.

and wealthy towns and villages. The Usk and Wye were renowned salmon rivers until two decades ago, this alone brings an air of prosperity to the area.

Affluence

The economic heart of the area still lies heavily with industry and the associated services that the main towns and the capital city provide. This brings a regular flow of visitors to the area with more emphasis on business than leisure. Facilities for visitors have improved markedly in the last decade with new hotels, conference and sporting centres being built. New golf courses include the magnificent Celtic Manor Resort and several in the Vale of Glamorgan. These all offer the finest accommodation, conference, spa, catering and leisure facilities. The increasing affluence of the area has attracted new designer retail outlets, speciality food shops and local food markets. Numerous restaurants and gastro

pubs have opened, serving quality produce only before seen in the most exclusive places. Many companies have grown to cater for the food service requirements of the area, and more speciality producers have established to cater for the high population of the area.

South East Wales: food of the area

Really Welsh fresh cauliflowers from the Vale of Glamorgan.

Penderyn Distillery is nestled in the foothills of the Brecon Beans mountain range. It is the only distillery in Wales and one of the smallest distilleries in the world.

N S James butchers is a rare meats specialist producing their own faggots, sausages and beef burgers. They also make a range of preserves and chutneys which they sell from their shop.

Food processing

The area from Port Talbot to Chepstow and north to the Heads of the Valleys road would not be considered important for primary production apart from the Vale of Glamorgan and Monmouthshire. It is, however, the heart of food manufacturing with far more companies based in the region than any other. The immediacy of the market and the proximity to distribution routes to London and the Midlands make this the most significant place for employment in the food industry.

The entire spectrum of food production, service and catering is found in this area. It is the most highly populated area of Wales with the most structured economy. In South East Wales the catering and food service plays the major role in the food industry. Second is food manufacturing with the smallest activity being primary and agriculture.

Some very large food manufacturers such as Peters Food Service and R F Brookes have state-of-the-art manufacturing premises. They might not necessarily use primary Welsh produce unless stated in lines such as Welsh Lamb Shepherds Pie. The same could well apply to many of the other pie, faggot and cooked food manufacturers such as Lewis Fine Foods of Pyle. Many of their products are made to traditional family or Welsh recipes and their production kitchens or factories are in Wales and they employ many local people.

Food manufacturing companies that utilise Welsh primary produce, whether meat, dairy foods or vegetables, partly or wholly in their processing, are the smaller or medium-sized operators. The Authentic Curry Company does market Welsh Black beef and Welsh lamb curry. Abergavenny Fine Foods use Welsh goats' milk in their range. Castle Dairies of Caerphilly utilise organic milk from Wales.

Baking

A large sector of the baking industry, particularly the small to medium companies, make products with a truly Welsh empathy such as bara brith and Welsh cakes. Many make bread to original styles such as a Swansea loaf, bara gwenith, bara planc, and sweet products such as teisen lap and Eve's pudding. Welsh branding on products such as oat cakes and shortbread emphasises their manufacturing origin such as the range from Welsh Hills Bakery.

Continental

There are many very interesting companies that make up a wide and diverse range of foods. Gorno's Speciality Foods make a range of Italian and Continental charcuterie to family recipes brought from Italy during the late nineteenth century. It was originally made for the Welsh Italian population but now is distributed nationally to the retail and catering industry. The Italian families of the Welsh valleys are entrenched in the food and catering industry as ice cream manufacturers, coffee roasters and merchants, café and restaurant owners.

Drinks

The drinks industry in this area has never suffered from a shortage of demand. Brewers and soft drink companies have a ready market that was traditionally in the mining valleys, seaside resorts and the main towns and cities. Brains Brewery, owned by the Cardiff family, is still situated close to the heart of the city having moved from its original premises a few years ago. Cardiff is the only city in the world where the main brewery and the sports stadium are in the heart of the city. Brains own a large number of pubs throughout Cardiff and now are expanding through Wales. Their range of cask conditioned and premium bottled beers is totally in line with current market trends and the brand goes from strength to strength.

This corner of Wales is the sunniest and warmest area and there is evidence of vineyards at Sully in the early 1900s. In the last 30 years a number of small vineyards have become established in the Vale and Monmouthshire. Sugarloaf, Monnow Valley, Parva, Llanerch, and Glyndŵr vineyards have all been established for over 20 years and each now produces a small range of wines, mainly white from Germanic grape varieties. A small amount of red, rosé and sparkling is made by some.

The Welsh Whisky Company is based at Penderyn, near Hirwaun, is on the border of south and mid Wales, near the boundary between Rhondda Cynon Taff and Powys. The Penderyn Single Malt Whisky is the first to be distilled in Wales for over a century. The Celtic Spirit Company produce a whisky liqueur, Danzi Jones, made to a local Welsh family recipe of herbs and berries blended with grain whisky.

Real pork from breeds such as Middlewhite or Old Spot, where animals are reared naturally, is something quite different and flavoursome.

Farmers' markets

Primary production of meat, milk and vegetables in the Vale of Glamorgan is on a more limited scale than the rest of Wales. Nevertheless a visit to any farmers' market will show the number of dedicated smaller producers who exist happily in the niche market. Pork, beef, lamb, poultry, venison and other game in season feature regularly. Monmouthshire is a county of finest agricultural land and the same range of produce is on a bigger scale. In both areas game is important on the big estates for the sporting market.

The range of fruit and vegetables that can be grown in the area covers from mushrooms to tomatoes with greens and winter roots following. Fruit farms in the vale have combined with local skills of ice cream making with good results.

Fishing

The rivers flowing into the Bristol Channel all have runs of salmon in season. The Ogmore, Taff, Usk, and Wye (particularly the latter two) have been important fisheries in the past. The Severn Estuary and Bristol Channel have fishing grounds that have all the regular species though local exploitation of these is not very active. The estuaries of all the rivers have an annual migration of baby eels (elvers) back to their mother river. Netting these as they battle their way up-river can be highly lucrative as the price they now fetch on Continental and far Eastern markets can be astronomic. Trapping mature eels as they migrate back to sea in the autumn was a lucrative way of fishing. A number of small trawlers operate from Cardiff, Newport, Barry, and Porthcawl. Most operate for recreational angling parties.

The Rivers Wye and Usk were both salmon rivers of great renown. The Wye was the most important salmon river south of Scotland. Catches to the rods alone were in the region of 8,000 fish a season into the 1980s. This was alongside commercial

The Riverside Market in Cardiff is one of the most popular markets with a host of produce from all across South Wales.

fishing in the estuary, the contribution to the economy was considerable, with numerous hotels and restaurants catering for anglers throughout the season. Catches are now under a quarter of the 1980s level and restrictions on fishing that aim to regenerate stocks have led to a big decline in this activity. Many other rivers have seen a decline in fishing activity for salmon, brown trout and sewin.

The sad decline of salmon is not only due to the lack of water quality on spawning rivers. Over the years the species has been over exploited in many ways. Poaching on the Wye and other rivers reached ridiculous proportion without any effective control. Now farmed salmon is widely available the value of the fish is a little lower and it's less worthwhile to poach the dwindled stocks.

Fishing for salmon between the polar ice cap and Britain has increased immensely in the last 30 years, so the number of fish returning to spawn has further declined.

Netting off the coast of Ireland and Wales also has taken its toll on salmon. Commercial fishing for sand eels to make food for fish farms has denied other fish, particularly sewin and bass their natural food and stocks of these have decreased considerably.

South East Wales: where to eat

SUPPLIERS

f Lamb ~ Brian George, Talgarth

son ~ Welsh Venison Centre, Bwlch

k ~ Madgettes Farm, Tidenham

k ~ Bower Farm, Grosmont & Stoney Barn, G-

ured Meats ~ Bellota, Orcop

Seasonal Game ~ William

Fish ~ Richard Gafney, Abergavenn

Smoked Salmon ~ Black Mountain

Trolway Brook Farm, Gar

t ~ Bower Farm, G

Graig, Ne

Only ingredients of the highest quality are used at the Hardwick to produce simple food well cooked.

A sample of the suppliers used by the Bell at Skenfrith.

Hearty home cooking at the Bell at Skenfrith.

Angel Hotel, Abergavenny

This Georgian town hotel has been refurbished in traditional style over the last several years. A spacious bar bistro and more formal restaurant serve wide ranging menus using much local produce. Black Mountain smoked salmon, Llanarth pheasant, Free-range chicken and pork, local Welsh lamb and beef and regularly delivered seafood are turned around in fine style by the competent kitchen team.
15 Cross Street, Abergavenny NP7 5EN
T: 01873 857121
E: info@angel-hotel.com
www.angel-hotel.com

Armless Dragon, Cardiff

This neighbourhood restaurant close to the city centre has the top reputation for its dedication to provenance of Welsh produce. Fish and shellfish are bought directly from boats in Pembrokeshire, while poultry and game is sourced from farms in Monmouthshire. Skilful cooking and eye catching presentations in generous portions set this ahead of most in the area.
97 – 99 Wyeverne Road, Cathays,
Cardiff CF24 4BG
T: 029 2038 2357
E: paul@thearmlessdragon.fsnet.co.uk
www.armlessdragon.co.uk

Bell at Skenfrith

Beautifully located on the River Dore this large pub restaurant with rooms has a judicious mix of contemporary and traditional décor. The same applies to the food that's served in this relaxed setting. Local suppliers are listed; some of the food even comes from the pub's garden. Some simpler traditional dishes are joined by those with eclectic touches that are popular along with the splendid wine list.
Skenfrith, Monmouthshire NP7 8UH
T: 01600 750235
E: enquiries@skenfrith.co.uk
www.skenfrith.co.uk

Black Bear, Bettws Newydd

Proprietor-cooked hearty food in a traditional country pub with character.
Bettws Newydd, Abergavenny NP15 1JN
T: 01873 880701

Blue Anchor Inn, East Aberthaw

This wonderful old pub has been rebuilt after a disastrous fire and retains the charm and character.
East Aberthaw CF62 3DD
T: 01446 750329
www.blueanchoraberthaw.com

Bunch of Grapes, Pontypridd

This gastro pub is a great find in a traditional valleys house. The menu has many Welsh ingredients taking in Talgarth ham, wood pigeon and Welsh meats, plus bass, crab and laverbread. Imaginative cooking might deliver crisp-fried lambs' sweetbreads, crayfish bisque, crab and cockle risotto and pigeon with wild mushrooms. There is a huge mixed grill for trenchermen.
Ynysangharad Road, Pontypridd CF3 4DA
T: 01443 402934
E: info@bunchofgrapes.org.uk
www.bunchofgrapes.org.uk

Caesars Arms, Creigiau

This huge country pub has the steak and fish counter formula with a central open kitchen.
Cardiff Road, Creigiau, near Llantrisant CF15 9NN
T: 029 2089 0486

Casanova, Cardiff

Convenient for the Millennium Stadium is this tiny authentic Italian-British eaterie.
13 Quay Street, Cardiff CF10 1EA
T: 029 2034 4044

Michelin-starred chef James Sommerin at work in The Crown at Whitebrook. This colourful terrine signifies the high level of contemporary cuisine enjoyed.

Matt Tebutt at the Foxhunter offers the verys best of modern British cuisine using recipes that remain true to the flavours of fresh, seasonal ingredients.

Chandlery, Newport

The handsome grade II listed building now houses a sleek modern restaurant. The skilled young team produce a menu showing a wide range of culinary techniques with quality ingredients. Smoked haddock scotch egg is novel and deep-fried telaggio a new play on a favourite. Trealy Farm pork, Middlewood venison and Welsh lamb have the house style with individual vegetables and garnishes. Desserts are mouthwatering.
77 – 78 Lower Dock Street, Newport NP20 1EH
T: 01633 256622
www.chandleryrestaurant.co.uk

Clytha Arms, Raglan

This unpretentious family-run country pub with rooms and restaurant retains its character. Confident cooking produces dishes with real traditional and cosmopolitan flavours. Seasonal menus feature cockles, laverbread, oysters, charcuterie followed by game pudding, teriyaki beef and roast pheasant. Enticing tapas in the bar include grilled clams, sardines, Carmarthen ham and chorizo to go with real ales, cider and reasonable wines.
Clytha, near Abergavenny NP7 9BW
T: 01873 840206
E: clythaarms@tiscali.co.uk
www.clytha-arms.com

Coast, Porthcawl

Local seafood, meat and game in season feature on a menu that changes regularly through the year.
2 – 4 Dock Street, Porthcawl CF36 3BL
T: 01656 782025
www.coastrestaurants.co.uk

Court Colman, Bridgend

A combined Indian and French brasserie in a grand country house hotel.
Pen-Fai, Bridgend CF31 4NG
T: 01656 720212
E: experience@court-colman-manor.com
www.court-colman-manor.com

The Crown at Celtic Manor

The combination of the Crown at Whitebrook's culinary brilliance and the grand setting of the Celtic Manor adds the final sophistication to this great resort hotel. Innovative use of fine Welsh and cosmopolitan ingredients comes across in stunning presentations and judicious balances of flavours and textures.
Coldra Woods, Newport NP18 1HQ
T: 01633 413000
www.celtic-manor.com

Crown at Whitebrook

In a secluded location in the lower Wye Valley, this Michelin-starred 'auberge' is now at the cutting edge of contemporary cuisine. The youthful team are dedicated to intricate dishes to bring out the best aspects of ingredients, perhaps pork cheek, squab pigeon, butternut squash, bass, venison and lamb. Sirloin with langoustine tortellini or turbot with belly pork show exciting flavour combinations. Truffles, mousses, soufflés and espuma feature on the dessert menu. An eight course 'degustation' is available nightly. A culinary experience.
Whitebrook, near Monmouth NP25 4TX
T: 01600 860254
E: info@crownatwhitebrook.co.uk
www.crownatwhitebrook.co.uk

Egerton Grey, Rhoose

This imposing country house hotel has splendid antiques and original features blended with beautifully refurbished individually designed rooms. Country house cuisine is served on elegant china. Dinner might include bass, lobster, turbot and John Dory, with Breconshire lamb and Welsh black beef. Lunches have lighter dishes and there is a popular Sunday lunch menu with a selection of hearty roasts.
Porthkerry, Rhoose, near Cardiff CF62 3BZ
T: 01446 711666
E: info@egertongrey.co.uk
www.egertongrey.co.uk

Stephen Terry busy in the Hardwick.

Foxhunter, Nantyderry

The well refurbished stationmaster's house has contemporary elegance and a pedigree kitchen. Masterful techniques come across in the use of European styles and ingredients melded with top rate seasonal local fare. A spring menu might include lambs' sweetbreads, smoked eel, Cornish lobster, sea trout, spring lamb, Middle White pork and Longhorn beef. Cooking is accurate and presentations artistic. Comfortable rooms encourage total indulgence.
Nantyderry, Abergavenny NP7 9DN
T: 01873 881101 E: info@thefoxhunter.com
www.thefoxhunter.com

Frolics, Southerndown

Flavoursome cuisine comes from the youthful team in this popular country destination.
Beach Road, Southerndown, near Bridgend CF32 0RP
T: 01656 880127

● True Taste
Award winners

Gilby's, Cardiff

This large converted barn restaurant with open kitchen serves tasty international food from fish and chips to intricate continental dishes with colourful garnishes.
Old Port Road, Culverhouse Cross, Cardiff CF5 6DN
T: 029 2067 0800
E: gilbysrestaurant@btconnect.com
www.gilbysrestaurant.co.uk

Gilby's @ the Bay, Cardiff

The link with the Cardiff restaurant has elevated standards with novel use of local produce. Welsh lamb, Usk Beef, Gower crab and Welsh cheese feature on the well balanced menu.
Wales Millennium Centre, Bute Place, Cardiff CF10 5AL
T: 029 2045 9000
E: enquiries@gilbysthebay.co.uk
www.enquiries@gilbysthebay.co.uk

Great House, Laleston

This magnificent historic country house hotel has up-to-date facilities for guests with flamboyant cuisine and a fine wine list.
High Street, Laleston, Bridgend CF32 0HP
T: 01656 657644
www.great-house-laleston.co.uk

Hardwick, Abergavenny ●

This former roadhouse pub is now a serious modern brasserie with top quality food from a renowned team. The long menu has simpler offerings lunchtime. House specialities are based on prime ingredients including Gloucester Old Spot, Brixham lobster and crab, Longhorn beef and Welsh lamb. These might come with accompaniments such as Amalfi lemons, cala negro cabbage and dandelions in masterful dishes.
Old Raglan Road, Abergavenny NP7 9AA
T: 01873 854220
E: info@thehardwick.co.uk
www.thehardwick.co.uk

Hare & Hounds, Aberthin
Traditional pub with great ales and true bar food in rural style.
Aberthin, near Cowbridge CF71 7HB
T: 01446 774892

Huddarts, Cowbridge
This pristine town house restaurant serves family-cooked imaginative cuisine.
69 High Street, Cowbridge CF71 7AF
T: 01446 774645

Inn at the Elm Tree, Wentlooge
This beautiful large inn in a secluded location on the estuary marshes has a reputation for well prepared food in a delightful contemporary dining room.
St Brides, Wentlooge, near Newport NP10 8SQ
T: 01633 680225
www.the-elm-tree.co.uk

Junction 28, Newport
This most popular restaurant has a wide choice of traditional and European cooking in appealing dishes.
Station Approach, Bassaleg, Newport NP10 8LD
T: 01633 891891

Kemeys Manor, Newport
Modern Italian influences on traditional cooking with fine Italian wines in a historic country house.
Kemeys Inferior, Caerleon NP18 1JS
T: 01633 450402
E: allison@kemeysmanor.com

La Fosse, Cardiff
Stylish cellar restaurant on broken levels with a seafood counter and fresh steaks served grilled, baked or deep fried.
9 – 11 The Hayes, Cardiff CF10 1AH
T: 02920 237755

La Marina & El Puerto, Penarth
This vast eaterie on Penarth Marina has the very reliable self-selected meats and seafood cooked simply on *la parilla* formula, plus fine dining in its upstairs restaurant. A Champagne bar and an amazing wine cellar set the tone for relaxed enjoyable dining with professional efficient service. Enjoy oysters, scallops, rock-salt-baked bass, well-matured steaks and grilled Welsh lamb.
Custom House, Penarth Marina, Penarth CF64 1TT
T: 029 2070 5551

Le Gallois, Cardiff
This longstanding gourmet haunt is noted for its ménage of classical French and Welsh culinary style. This has developed with an original tapas and Welsh breakfast menus. The express lunch has been applauded for its quality and value, while evenings have well established dinner specialities. Accuracy and fine balance of flavours throughout mark out the skilled cuisine.
6 – 10 Romilly Crescent, Canton, Cardiff CF11 9NR
T: 029 2034 1264 E: info@legallois-ycymro.com
www.legallois-ycymro.com

Le Monde, Cardiff
Renowned for being the best seafood restaurant in the area, with counters full of glistening produce. This huge restaurant complex takes in Champers and La Brasserie.
62 St Mary Street, Cardiff CF10 1FE
T: 029 2038 7376

Llansantffraed Court, near Abergavenny
This fine country mansion in beautiful grounds is renowned for magnificent wedding parties. The same competent cooking comes through in the spacious hotel restaurant. Many Welsh ingredients and specialities feature on the menu.
Llanvihangel Gobion, Abergavenny, Monmouthshire NP7 9BA
T: 01873 840678

Established for 10 years Le Gallois has a reputation for good food and service which has gained critical acclaim in regional and national press.

Llanwenarth Arms, Abergavenny

A large restaurant with rooms on the banks of the Usk catering for big numbers in considerable style.
Brecon Road, Abergavenny NP8 1EP
T: 01873 810550

Newbridge Inn, Tredunnock

This large country pub with superb boutique style rooms serves a varied fresh seafood menu from Cornwall and a large selection of lamb beef and poultry dishes.
Tredunnock, near Usk, Monmouthshire, NP15 1LY
T: 01633 451000
E: eatandsleep@thenewbridge.co.uk
www.thenewbridge.co.uk

Old Post Office, St Fagans

The façade from the road hides the elegant minimalist décor that gives a tranquil air to this restaurant with rooms.

Cooking is soundly based on experience and knowledge of ingredients. There is an Italian influence in many dishes from seasonal ingredients such as Brecon beef, Welsh lamb, partridge, bass and halibut. Ham hock terrine and truffled risotto cake show the breadth of flavours to expect.
Greenwood Lane, St Fagans, Cardiff CF5 6EL
T: 029 2056 5400
E: info@theoldpostofficerestaurant.co.uk
www.theoldpostofficerestaurant.co.uk

Park Plaza, Cardiff

This smart hotel has a modern brasserie with well prepared seafood and meat dishes featuring much Welsh produce.
Park Plaza Hotel, Greyfriars Road, Cardiff CF10 3AL
T: 029 2011 1101
www.parkplaza.com

Patagonia, Cardiff

This popular restaurant serves light meals throughout the day and grows into a full restaurant with an interesting menu evenings. The mix of South American cooking and Welsh ingredients makes some very tasty dishes with delicious Patagonian wines.
11 Kings Road, Cardiff CF11 9BZ
T: 029 2019 0265
www.patagonia-restaurant.co.uk

Plough & Harrow, Monknash

A great country pub for hearty food, real ales and reasonably priced wines.
Monknash, near Cowbridge CF71 7QQ
T: 01656 890209
E: info@theploughmonknash.com
www.theploughmonknash.com

Prego, Monmouth

Locally sourced seasonal food gives a stamp of quality to this town-centre restaurant with rooms. Italian influences and Welsh ingredients bring an exciting range of dishes to the unpretentious setting.

7 Church Street, Monmouth NP25 3BX
T: 01600 712600
www.pregomonmouth.co.uk

The Priory Hotel, Caerleon

This large restaurant has the steak and seafood counter to grill formula. Accommodation has some suites and more basic comfortable rooms.
High Street, Caerleon NP18 1AG
T: 01633 421241

Razzi, Cardiff

In the well located modern Hilton hotel informal dining is in a café-brasserie facing the Cardiff Castle wall.
Hilton Hotel, 1 Kingsway, Cardiff CF10 3HH
T: 029 2064 6400

Red Lion, Pendoylan

Beautiful country pub with French style cooking from many local ingredients.
Pendoylan CF71 7UJ
T: 01446 760332

Stonemill, Rockfield, near Monmouth

Accommodation is in pristine farm style cottages and enjoyable dining in a beautifully renovated barn with some Welsh – Italian dishes.
Rockfield, near Monmouth NP25 5SW
T: 01600 716273
E: bookings@thestonemill.co.uk
www.thestonemill.co.uk

Thai House, Cardiff

Tasty family-produced Thai dishes using some Welsh meat and seafood.
3-5 Guildford Crescent, Churchill Way, Cardiff CF10 2HJ
T: 029 2038 7404
www.thaihouse.biz

Tides, Cardiff

In the luxurious St David's hotel dine in the stylish restaurant overlooking the lagoon of Cardiff Bay.
St Davids Hotel, Havannah Street, Cardiff CF10 5SD
T: 029 2045 4045

Twenty Four, Monmouth

This little restaurant has some sophisticated dishes that show a high level of creativity and skill. Real home cooking with provenance of ingredients has hearty soups, braised dishes, pork loaf with chips, alongside perhaps chargrilled meats and baked fish. Some sumptuous desserts and reasonable wines make this a favourite in the old part of town.
24 Church Street, Monmouth NP25 3BU
T: 01600 772744

Walnut Tree, Llanddewi Skirrid

This much-loved restaurant has re-opened with a highly skilled team that aims to restore its former glory. Modern culinary techniques are applied to traditional ingredients, whether seafood, game, poultry, meat and offal. Everything through to desserts is presented in dishes with immense flavour and harmony.
Llanddewi Skirrid, near Abergavenny NP7 8AW
T: 01873 852797
www.thewalnuttreeinn.com

Woods Brasserie, Cardiff

This favourite modern brasserie has contemporary style cooking with international influences.
The Pilotage Building, Stuart Street, Cardiff Bay CF10 5BW
T: 029 2049 2400
www.woods-brasserie.com

South East Wales: where to buy and producers

USK WILD BOAR
&
CRANBERRY
SAUSAGES

Made with local wild boar, the
meaty taste is complemented
with the slightly sweet berries

per kg £6.50
per lb £2.95

Strawberries from the Vale of Glamorgan, Monmouthshire and Wye Valley are sold at food festivals and farmers' markets in the summer months.

A selection of free range pork and wild boar sausages from R K Palfrey.

South East Wales has a number of vineyards producing white and rose wines including the award-winning Cariad from Llanerch Vineyard.

The prosperous South East

The south east area is the smallest yet the most densely populated in Wales. The capital city Cardiff not only has the administrative role but also has a most vibrant and prosperous business community. Its influence reaches far out into the Welsh valleys, the Vale of Glamorgan and Monmouth. The prosperity generated gives this area the most powerful spending capacity and the structure of the food wholesale and retail industry is geared accordingly. All the multiples are found throughout the region competing for the business in every town and village. Alongside this there are many smaller independent retailers and food markets that give the consumer a choice of where to buy local Welsh produce.

Food festivals

The most popular food festival in Wales is held annually at Abergavenny. It has become somewhat of a cult festival as well as a place for all Welsh producers to exhibit and sell their wares. Activities reach beyond this to food tastings, demonstrations, discussions and debates with food celebrities giving lectures on current and trendy food topics. Restaurants and bars put on special menus and several grand functions make it the social food event of the year.

Cardiff is host to a major festival held in the Roald Dahl Plass in Cardiff Bay. It has now developed into The Cardiff International Food and Drink Festival in line with the status of the cosmopolitan city. Elsewhere entertainment is on-going with the French contingent of Les Chevaliers des Bretvins joining with the Welsh confrerie for wine and food tastings, ceremonies and dinners.

The Cowbridge Food Festival has developed into another major event with more of a local emphasis of food from the Vale. The event takes over the whole of the town with events in several venues and food demonstrations and entertainment.

Real fun can be had at the cheese, beer and cider festivals held at the Clytha Arms on Spring and August bank holidays.

Produce markets

Farmers and local produce markets are held throughout the area as there is no shortage of people willing to pay for food with true provenance. Farmers, smallholders, artisan producers and traders from the Vale of Glamorgan, Monmouthshire and beyond attend many of the markets of the area and have built up a local following. The Cardiff Riverside Market has become a cosmopolitan eating day out with numerous restaurants cooking all kinds of food for grazing as people tour the stalls. Pâté producers, bakers, organic poultry, meat and vegetable farmers and farmhouse cheesemakers all join in the ambience of the event. Other markets of the area include Penarth, Roath, Abergavenny, Monmouth and Usk to less likely venues such as Merthyr Tydfil and Tonypandy which demonstrates the popularity of these markets.

Cardiff's Central Market has some of the finest traders of long standing. The fish shop Ashtons at the Hayes entrance has one of the finest displays of fresh seafood including much local stuff. Whereas species such as cod, hake, halibut, salmon and haddock in its fresh or cured state would come from the east coast or Scotland, there is line caught bass from Pembroke, cockles, mussels and laverbread from Gower, and game from Monmouthshire. Traditional fruit and vegetable stalls and a row of independent butchers, including J P Morgan, make this a popular destination. There are more modest markets at Bridgend and Abergavenny.

Rural shopping

The rolling countryside of Monmouthshire has a rural heritage that has developed into a very sophisticated area, with wealthy and busy towns such as Usk, Raglan,

Abergavenny, Crickhowell and Monmouth. The area has a food culture unlike anywhere else in Wales with many top restaurants, and the prosperity is reflected in the number of highly successful independent butchers, fine food shops and farm gate shops. Abergavenny has Rawlings and Edwards as independent butchers. The Tredilion Fruit Farm and Glan Usk Estate are both close by. Around Monmouth town, Carrob Growers and Hancocks Butchers make very good shopping.

Raglan has James Butchers with Cefn Maen and Brooks shops close by. Newport has RK Palfrey one of the master butchers of the area and distinguished member of the Guild of Butchers.

Delicatessens

Delicatessens have a loyal following in Cardiff and surrounding area. Thyme Out in Dinas Powys, Wild Fig Farm Foods in Peterston-super-Ely, Foxy's Deli in Penarth, Farthings at Home in Cowbridge all benefit from the prosperity in the Vale. In Cardiff Wally's Delicatessen in the Royal Arcade is an institution and akin to entering an Aladdin's cave of gourmet delights. Also visit the Rowan Tree delicatessen in Cathays terrace.

For a real selection of Welsh produce visit the Gwalia Stores in the St Fagans National History Museum. It is set out as a traditional grocer of the type that used to be found in many towns and villages. Also visit the Dderwen Bakery with its wood burning oven using local birch as fuel. Sample and buy their selection of bread from stone ground flour, Welsh cakes, bara brith, pasties, and a range of sweet and savouries that melt in the mouth.

Welsh wine

The vineyards of the area all sell from their own shops. The largest is the Llanerch Vineyard known for its Cariad wine in white, rosé and sparkling. They now have a café-bar-restaurant with cookery school attached, as well as self catering cottages and a swimming pool. Close to Abergavenny the Sugarloaf Vineyard sells their delicious white wines from the shop. The Glyndŵr Vineyard at Llanblethian, and Parva Vineyard, Tintern have shops open most days. The Celtic Spirit Company, makers of Danzy Jones Wysgi Licor, Celtic Poteen and Black Mountain Liqueur sell from their depot in Abergavenny and in many shops throughout the area.

The name Vin Sullivan is renowned throughout the county as one of the largest stockists of Welsh produce for the catering industry. This, alongside their vast range of international foods can provide literally everything for the caterer. Their purpose built unit in Blaenavon now has a retail shop that has immediate access to the rich stocks in the warehouse. The company trawls Wales for everything available including fish and shellfish from the coast; the best Welsh meats from salt marsh lamb to finest sausages; game from the estates covering all in fur-and-feather in season; pâtés, pies, cured cooked products; smoked fish and meat; vegetables and fruit; bakery goods and patisserie; and the widest selection of Welsh cheese from larger firms to the smallest artisan producers to be found.

Welsh whisky

Something to enjoy in an armchair is the first Welsh whisky to be produced for a century. The newly opened visitor centre at The Welsh Whisky Co in Penderyn is on the south of the Brecon Beacons. It shows the process from mashing the barley, the distillation through to maturation in oak casks and bottling. A whole variety of presentations and ages can be purchased in the shop together with other spirits and Welsh specialities.

● True Taste
  Award winners

markets, shops, specialists and producers in South East Wales

Abergavenny Fine Foods
Cheese manufacturers, flavoured cheese and cheese snacks.
Castle Meadows Park, Abergavenny NP7 7RZ
T: 01873 850001
E: enquiries@abergavenny.uk.com

Abergavenny Market
Town market with traditional producers and retailers.
Market Office, Town Hall, Cross Street, Abergavenny NP7 5HD
T: 01873 735811

Ashton (Fishmongers)
High quality fishmonger and game dealer.
Cardiff Central Market, St Mary Street, Cardiff CF10 1AU
T: 029 2022 9201

Authentic Curry Company
Manufacturer of dishes for food service using local meat and authentic recipes.
Unit 46/47, Hirwaun Industrial Estate, Hirwaun CF44 9UP
T: 01685 810044
E: paul.trotman@authenticcurry.co.uk

Baldocks, Newport
Meats, cheeses, pies, olives, pâtés, continental beers and fine wines.
Newport Market, Newport NP20 1DD
T: 01633 257312
www.baldocks-deli.co.uk

Blaenavon Cheddar ●
Cheese matured underground in former coal mine.
80 Broad Street, Blaenafon NP4 9NF
T: 01495 793123
www.chunkofcheese.co.uk

Bridgend Indoor Market
Town market with traditional producers and retailers.
Market Hall, Rhiw Shopping Centre, Bridgend CF31 3BL

Brooks Farm
Traditional farm shop sourcing local produce.
Chepstow Road, Raglan NP15 2HX
T: 01291 690319

C & G Morgan & Son
High quality meat from traditional farm.
Gelli Feddgaer Farm, Blackmill, Bridgend CF35 6EN
T: 01443 672357

Capital Cuisine
Outside catering specialists and quality food manufacturers.
123 Pandy Road, Bedwas, Caerphilly CF83 8EL
T: 07957 422546
www.capitalcuisine.co.uk

Carrob Growers
Small specialist vegetable grower.
Llangunville, Llanrothal, Monmouth NP25 5QL
T: 01600 712451

Cardiff Central Market
City market with traditional mix of food and general traders.
St Mary Street, Cardiff CF10 1AU
T: 029 2087 1214
E: enquiries@cardiff-market.co.uk
www.cardiff-market.co.uk

Castle Dairies
Cheese, milk and butter from locally sourced and organic suppliers.
Pontygwindy Industrial Estate, Caerphilly CF83 3HU
T: 029 2088 3981
E: norman@castledairies.co.uk
www.castledairies.co.uk

● True Taste
　Award winners

Cefn Maen Farm
Free-range organic bronze turkeys for the Christmas market.
Cefn Maen Farm, Usk Road, Raglan NP15 2HR
T: 01291 690428

Celtic Spirit Co
Traditional local recipes for spirits and liqueurs.
1 Castle Meadows Park, Merthyr Road, Abergavenny NP7 7RZ
T: 01873 735770
E: sales@celticspirit.co.uk
www.celticspirit.co.uk

Cig Mynydd Cymru ●
Free-range pork from farms on the Black Mountains.
16b Perrott Street, Treharris CF46 5ER
T: 01443 41319
www.cigmynyddcymru.co.uk

Cwrt Henllys Farm
Quality rare-breed meat from own farm.
Henllys, Cwmbran NP44 7AS
T: 01633 612349
www.cwrthenllysfarm.co.uk

Cwrt Newydd Vegetarian Produce
Vegetarian ready made dishes and snacks.
Cwrt Newydd, Aberthin, Cowbridge CF71 7HE
T: 01446 775240

Dderwen Bakehouse
Wood fired baking oven for daily bread and cakes to traditional style.
National History Museum, St Fagans, Cardiff CF5 6XB

Dyffryn Smoked Produce
Traditional style smoked meat and fish.
Beili-Mawr Home Farm, Dyffryn, Cardiff
T: 029 2059 9488

Farmhouse Freedom Eggs
High quality true free-range eggs.
Great House Farm, Gwehelog, near Usk NP15 1RJ
T: 01291 673129
E: sales@freedomeggs.co.uk
www.freedomeggs.co.uk

Farthings at Home
Delicatessen with home produced dishes as served in their wine bar.
31 High Street, Cowbridge CF71 7AE
T: 01446 773545
www.farthingsofcowbridge.co.uk

Food For Thought
Modern delicatessen with many Welsh specialities.
12 High Street, Barry CF62 7EA
T: 01446 735711

Foxy's Delicatessen
Quality delicatessen with comprehensive range and many local specialities.
7 Royal Buildings, Victoria Road, Penarth CF64 3ED
T: 029 2025 1666
www.foxysdeli.com

Glan Usk Farm Shop
Farm shop and PYO.
Llanfair Kilgeddin, Abergavenny NP7 9YE
T: 01873 880599

Glyndŵr Vineyard
White and red wine in Vale of Glamorgan.
Glyndŵr House, Llanblethian, Cowbridge CF71 7JF
T: 01446 774564
E: glyndwrvineyard@hotmail.com
www.glyndwrvineyard.co.uk

Gorno's Speciality Foods
Traditional Italian charcuterie for retail and catering market.
Unit 3, Fairfield Industrial Estate, Mair Road, Gwaelod-y-Garth, Cardiff CF15 8LA
T: 029 2081 1225 E: gornos.foods@virgin.net
www.gornos.co.uk

Gwalia Stores
Old fashioned high street general food stores in Folk Museum.
National History Museum, St Fagans, Cardiff CF5 6XB
T: 029 2057 7018

Gwynt Y Ddraig Cider
Traditional cider from local apples.
Llest Farm, Llantwit Fardre, Pontypridd CF38 2PW
T: 01443 209852
www.gwyntcider.com

Hancocks of Monmouth
Independent butcher supplying local meats and award winning sausages for over a century
34 Monnow Street, Monmouth NP25 3EN
T: 01600 712015

H J Edwards & Son
Large scale independent butcher and delicatessen with in house bakery for pies, pasties and ready meals; all meat sourced within the area.
1–3, Flannel Street, Abergavenny NP7 5EG
T: 01873 853110

J P Morgan Butchers
True quality butcher in Cardiff Market.
Cardiff Central Market, St Mary Street, Cardiff CF10 1AU
T: 029 2034 1247

Le Gallois Deli
Modern delicatessen with many homemade specialities.
231 Cathedral Road, Cardiff CF11 9PP
T: 029 2035 483
E: info@legalloisdeli.com

Lewis Fine Foods
Traditional baker with many sweet and savoury specialities.
3 Heol Mostyn, Village Farm Industrial Estate, Pyle, Bridgend CF33 6BJ
T: 01656 749441
E: lewisfinefoods@btconnect.com
www.welshcake.co.uk

Llanerch Vineyard
Vineyard, wines, restaurant, self-catering accomodation and cookery school.
Hensol, Pendoylan CF72 8GG
T: 01443 225877
E: enquiries@llanerch-vineyard.co.uk
www.llanerch-vineyard.co.uk

M & D Embury
Farmers and family butchers with own cured meats.
Cadfor Farm, Govilon, Abergavenny NP7 9NU
T: 01873 853019

Medhope Organic Growers
Farm shop selling locally grown organic fruit and vegetables. Organic boxes to order.
Tintern, Monmouthshire NP16 7NX
T: 01291 689797

Monnow Valley Vineyards
Vineyard, white red and sparkling wines.
Great Osbaston Farm, Monmouth NP25 5DL
T: 01600 716209
E: wine@monnowvalley.com

N S James
Award winning family master butcher with home killed local meats and True Taste winning home cooked faggots.
Crown Square, Usk Rd, Raglan, Usk NP15 2EB
T: 01291 690675

Otley Brewing Company
Individual style ales from a small brewery.
Unit 42, Albion Industrial Estate, Pontypridd CF37 4NX
T: 01443 480555
E: info@otleybrewing.co.uk
www.otleybrewing.co.uk

Parva Vineyard
Wye valleyside vineyard and shop with white and rosé wines.
Tintern, Chepstow NP16 6SQ
T: 01291 689636
E: parvafarm@hotmail.com

True Taste
Award winners

Penllyn Estate Farm

Farm shop specialising in beef from estate.
Llwynhelig, Cowbridge CF71 7FF
T: 01446 772600

Peters Food Service

Large manufacturer for food service
industry.
Bedwas House Industrial Estate, Bedwas,
Caerphilly CF83 8XP
T: 029 2085 3200
E: info@petersfood.com
www.petersfood.com

Rawlings Family Butcher

Long standing perfectionist butcher
specialising in free range meat from local
farms.
19 Market Street, Abergavenny NP7 5SD
T: 01873 856773

Real Crisps (Sirhowy Valley Food)

Traditional crisps with many novel flavours.
17 -18 Willow Road, Pen-y-Fan Industrial
Estate, Crumlin, Newport NP11 4EG
T: 01495 241960
E: sales@realcrisps.com
www.realcrisps.com

Really Welsh

Leeks, daffodils and vegetables from
traditional farms.
Wick Road, Llantwit Major CF61 1YU
T: 01446 796386
www.reallywelsh.com

R F Brookes

Large food manufacturer of ready meals for
multiples.
Azalea Road, Rogerstone Park, Rogerstone
NP10 9SA
T: 01633 403000
www.brookesavana.co.uk

R K Palfrey, Newport ●

High quality butcher with finest product
sourcing.
36a Church Road, Newport NP19 7EL
T: 01633 259385
E: peter@rkpalfrey.co.uk
www.rkpalfrey.co.uk

Rowan Tree

Delicatessen with Welsh and continental
specialities.
141 Cathays Terrace, Cardiff CF24 4HW
T: 029 2039 7795
E: gill.durbin@rowantreedelicatessen.co.uk
www.rowantreedelicatessen.co.uk

S.A.Brain & Co

Traditional brewery in centre of Cardiff with
many public houses.
The Cardiff Brewery, PO Box 53,
Cardiff CF10 1SP
T: 029 2040 2094
www.sabrain.com

Serious Food Company ●

Specialist in high quality meals and desserts
for retail.
Unit 10, Llantrisant Business Park,
Llantrisant CF72 8LF
T: 01443 237222
E: info@seriousfood.co.uk
www.seriouslymmm.co.uk

Snails

Modern delicatessen with many Welsh
specialities.
6 Beulah Road, Rhiwbina, Cardiff CF14 6LX
T: 029 2062 0415
E: frangipanihome@hotmail.com

Sugarloaf Vineyards

White and rosé wines from mountain
vineyard.
Dummar Farm, Pentre Lane, Abergavenny
NP7 7LA
T: 01873 853066
www.sugarloafvineyards.co.uk

Thornhill Farm Shop
Farm shop with home grown specialities.
Capel Gwilyn Road, Thornhill, Cardiff
CF14 9UB
T: 029 2061 1707
E: thornhillfarmshop@googlemail.com
www.thornhillfarm.co.uk

Thyme Out Delicatessen
Traditional modern delicatessen with many
Welsh foods.
5 Elm Grove, Dinas Powys,
Vale of Glamorgan CF64 4AA
T: 029 2051 2200
E: mullanek55@hotmail.co.uk

Tredilion Fruit Farm
Seasonal fruit farm and PYO.
Llantilio Pertholey, Abergavenny NP7 8BG
T: 01873 854355

Ty Tanglwyst Dairy
Local milk sourced from area.
Pyle, Bridgend CF33 4SA
T: 01656 745635
www.tytanglwystdairy.com

Vin Sullivan
Large wholesaler of Welsh and international
foods with a state-of-the-art retail shop.
2 Gilchrist Thomas Estate, Blaenavon
NP4 9RL
T: 01495 796612 E: sales@vin-sullivan.co.uk
www.vin-sullivan.co.uk

Wally's Delicatessen
Traditional Italian salumeria with
international and some Welsh produce.
42 – 44 Royal Arcade, Cardiff CF10 1AE
T: 029 2022 9265
www.wallysdeli.co.uk

Welsh Hills Bakery
Biscuits and cakes to traditional recipes for
Welsh retailers.
Tramway, Hirwaun, Aberdare CF44 9NY
T: 01685 813545
E: sales@welshhills.com

Welsh Whisky Company
Wales's only distillery with single malt in
cask and bottle. Shop, tastings, tours.
Penderyn Distillery, Penderyn, near
Aberdare CF44 0SX
T: 01685 813300
E: info@welsh-whisky.co.uk
www.welsh-whisky.co.uk

Wild Fig Farm Foods
Seasonal fruit farm making own produce and
ices PYO.
Groes Faen Road, Peterston-Super-Ely,
Cardiff CF5 6NE
T: 01446 760358
E: enquires@wildfigfarm.co.uk
www.wildfigfarm.co.uk

seasonal timeline

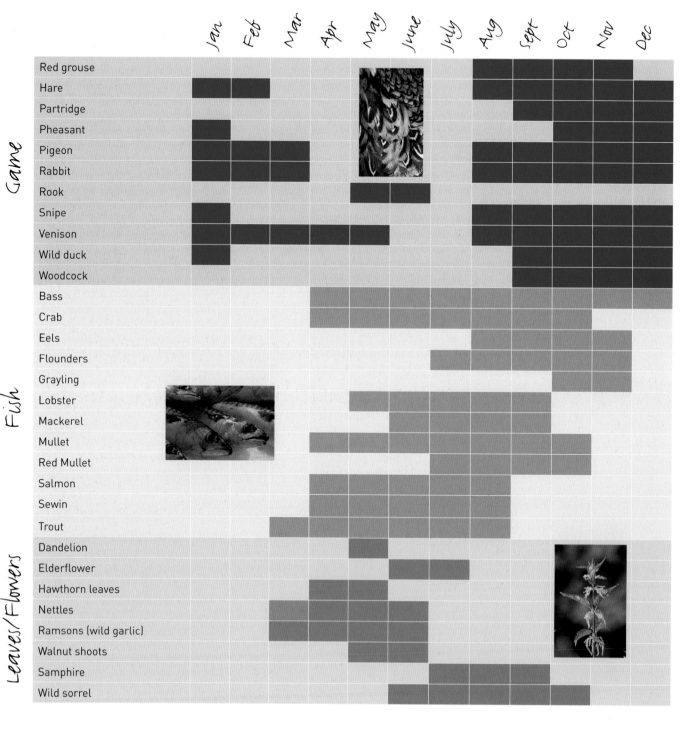

		Jan	Feb	Mar	Apr	May	June	July	Aug	Sept	Oct	Nov	Dec
Game	Red grouse								●	●	●	●	●
	Hare	●	●						●	●	●	●	●
	Partridge									●	●	●	●
	Pheasant	●									●	●	●
	Pigeon	●	●	●					●	●	●	●	●
	Rabbit	●	●	●					●	●	●	●	●
	Rook					●	●						
	Snipe	●	●						●	●	●	●	●
	Venison	●	●	●	●	●	●		●	●	●	●	●
	Wild duck	●								●	●	●	●
	Woodcock									●	●	●	●
Fish	Bass				●	●	●	●	●	●	●	●	●
	Crab				●	●	●	●	●	●	●	●	
	Eels								●	●	●	●	●
	Flounders							●	●	●	●	●	●
	Grayling										●	●	●
	Lobster					●	●	●	●	●	●		
	Mackerel				●	●	●	●	●	●	●	●	
	Mullet				●	●	●	●	●	●	●		
	Red Mullet					●	●	●	●	●			
	Salmon				●	●	●	●	●				
	Sewin				●	●	●	●	●				
	Trout			●	●	●	●	●	●	●			
Leaves/Flowers	Dandelion					●	●						
	Elderflower						●	●					
	Hawthorn leaves				●	●							
	Nettles			●	●	●	●						
	Ramsons (wild garlic)			●	●	●	●						
	Walnut shoots			●	●	●							
	Samphire							●	●	●	●		
	Wild sorrel					●	●	●	●	●	●		

Most food has a time when it is abundant and at its best. My seasonal timeline of Welsh food indicates when foods are in season. Use it to enjoy fish, fungi, nuts and berries at their freshest whilst helping to sustain local producers and our environment.

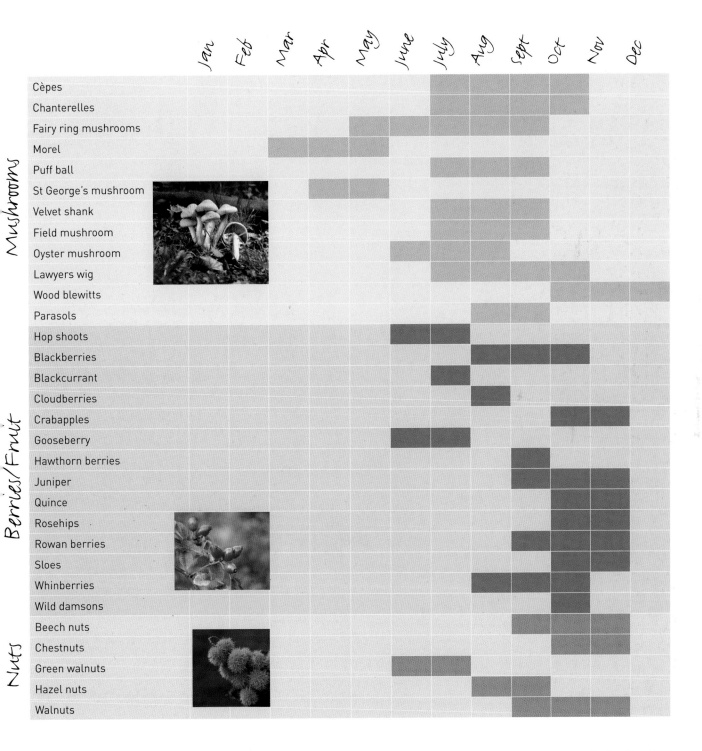

Mushrooms

	Jan	Feb	Mar	Apr	May	June	July	Aug	Sept	Oct	Nov	Dec
Cèpes							▓	▓	▓	▓		
Chanterelles								▓	▓	▓		
Fairy ring mushrooms					▓	▓	▓	▓				
Morel			▓	▓	▓							
Puff ball								▓	▓			
St George's mushroom				▓	▓							
Velvet shank								▓	▓			
Field mushroom								▓	▓			
Oyster mushroom							▓	▓	▓	▓		
Lawyers wig							▓	▓	▓	▓		
Wood blewitts										▓	▓	▓
Parasols												

Berries/Fruit

	Jan	Feb	Mar	Apr	May	June	July	Aug	Sept	Oct	Nov	Dec
Hop shoots						▓	▓					
Blackberries								▓	▓	▓		
Blackcurrant							▓					
Cloudberries								▓				
Crabapples										▓	▓	
Gooseberry						▓	▓					
Hawthorn berries									▓	▓		
Juniper									▓	▓	▓	
Quince										▓	▓	
Rosehips										▓	▓	
Rowan berries									▓	▓		
Sloes										▓	▓	
Whinberries								▓	▓			
Wild damsons										▓		

Nuts

	Jan	Feb	Mar	Apr	May	June	July	Aug	Sept	Oct	Nov	Dec
Beech nuts									▓	▓		
Chestnuts										▓	▓	
Green walnuts						▓	▓					
Hazel nuts									▓	▓		
Walnuts										▓	▓	

A-Z of
Welsh food

Salmon run in the Dee, Wye and other Welsh rivers. Their pinky-orange flesh is highly sought-after in top restaurants.

There are a number of different types of cattle bred in Wales and a growing demand for this meat to be traceable. This roast beef is from Llŷn.

Laver balls are made with oatmeal, seeds and laverbread – a traditional Welsh food.

Food from the sea

The coast of Wales benefits from the volume of the North Atlantic Ocean and the Gulf Stream that brings warm water to the shores. It has a wide tidal range; the Bristol Channel is second only to the Bay of Fundy in Canada. Hence there is a huge diversity of species found, many of which are seasonal.

The huge trawler fleets of Swansea and Milford Haven are no more. But these have been replaced by a large number of smaller inshore boats that moor in the numerous small harbours all around the coastline. The species caught has changed considerably over the years. Bass is now one of the most important fish landed in most areas of Wales, particularly Gower, Pembrokeshire and the Llŷn Peninsula.

Shellfish, particularly crab and lobster are important to fishing economies throughout. Re-stocking lobster programmes aimed at sustainability and other controls are in place throughout inshore fisheries. The cockle fishery at Penclawdd was the first in the world to be designated a sustainable fishery by the Marine Stewardship Council. One of the first marine reserves has been established in the Bristol Channel, above Lundy Island and already this is showing promising results with improved catches in areas around the reserve. The sound management of the mussel fishery in the Menai Straits makes this the largest mussel fishery in the British Isles with over 15,000 tonnes harvested annually. With continued effort and control the sustainability and future of many species and fisheries will be more secure.

Fish farming is developing in some areas but on a minute scale compared to Scotland. However, specific high-value species, such as turbot from the Blue Water Flatfish Farm on Anglesey, demonstrate the potential for the future.

shellfish

Cockle
This edible, small bi-valve sea mollusc or clam lives just below the surface of sand or mud, particularly in estuaries or sheltered beaches. They can be raked from the sand at low tide. They are harvested commercially at Penclawdd on Burry Estuary and the Three Rivers and sold fresh in markets and fishmongers; or bottled in vinegar. Seasonality all year.

Mussel
A deep blue bi-valve that attaches itself to shingle or rocks with a fine thread. They are harvested by hand in south Wales or by large commercial dredgers in North. Most popular served as 'moules marinière' steamed with white wine, herbs and shallots. Main season September – March.

Pacific Rock Oyster
Farmed in Britain, the spat or seed oysters are grown on mesh bags to commercial size in Wales in the Menai Straits. This elongated asymmetric bi-valve with creamy white firm flesh is the most popular shellfish to eat raw. Main season September – May.

Native Oyster
A flatter, rounder shell. They grow naturally and can be found in Swansea Bay and Milford Haven where fisheries thrived in the nineteenth century, but now not in commercial quantities. Main season September – May.

Prawn
Local prawns have only been fished in a small way until recently. Now they are caught using small pots similar to a

lobster pots with fine netting. Several boats fish for these in Cardigan Bay. Most are exported live in vivier lorries. The prawns most commonly used in restaurants are fished in the Northern Atlantic off Norway, Greenland, Iceland and America. Main season in Wales April – October.

Brown Crab

The brown crab is caught in pots similar to lobster pots, often as a bi-catch. Most are exported with lobsters, but in most areas there is a thriving cottage industry extracting the crabmeat to sell to local shops and the catering industry. In the Bristol Channel, particularly Gower and South Pembrokeshire they can be found on the rocks at low tide. Main season April – October.

Spider Crab

Very common in some areas particularly in the summer months. Some enlightened caterers and processors are now using this specie that was ignored until recently. The white flesh from the legs of the spider crab is particularly succulent. Main season April – September.

Velvet Crab

The velvet, swimming or fiddler crab is now exported live to continental markets for making fish soup and zarzuela (Spanish fish stew). Main season May – September.

Lobster

This is the most highly-prized specie from the sea. The heavily armoured crustacean turns orange red on cooking and has the most sweet and succulent white flesh. It is caught all around the Welsh coastline using baited pots. Lobster and crab can be caught using a crabbing hook and net in Gower and Pembroke where large stretches of rock are exposed on low spring tides. Main season May – September.

Crayfish

The spiny lobster with no claws is similar to those fished in tropical waters. The brown-red body is similar to a lobster's and consists of a rigid carapace and a flexible jointed tail that enables rapid swimming and escape. The white tail flesh is highly prized although all the carapace meat and legs are very delicious. They are caught off the Pembrokeshire coast either by divers or in lobster pots. Main season June – September.

Scallop

The distinctive fan shaped shell of the scallop is very familiar. One shell is concave, the other flat. The flesh of the muscle is succulent and creamy white with a bright orange roe. The remaining flesh is discarded. They are fished with dredges off Anglesey and in Cardigan Bay; some are hand-gathered by divers off Pembrokeshire. Main season October – May.

Queen Scallop

Similar to the scallop but smaller with two concave shells these might be fished with scallops. Their white flesh is equally tasty but do not have the firm, assertive texture of scallops. Main season October – May.

Winkle

These small sea snails are found on rocky areas in the intertidal zone. They have a distinctive green black spiral shell up to 3cm in size, with white interior and round operculum. They are gathered in many areas and mainly exported to France and Spain. A few are sold ready cooked in local markets such as on the cockle stalls in Swansea Market. The shellfish has to be soaked overnight in clean salted water to purge of grit and other material. They are then boiled in salted water (best with the addition of herbs and spices) for about five minutes. Main season March – October.

Whelk

These large sea snails are generally found below the low tide mark and are frequently caught as a bi-catch in lobster pots. The large spiral shall can be up to 10cm long. Fisheries have developed in North Wales for whelks using plastic baited pots with great success. These are purchased for processing and export to the Far Eastern markets. Whelk meat is sold in some markets alongside other shellfish, particularly at Swansea and Cardiff. Seasonality all year.

Fish

Angler/monkfish

This somewhat ugly fish catches smaller species by attracting them with a fin developed into an extended spine or fishing rod. It does have the most succulent flesh often compared to (but in no way as flavoursome as) lobster or prawn. The tail of the fish is well-textured firm and meaty. It has no bones being a cartilaginous specie and hence very popular. It is caught in trawler nets particularly in Pembrokeshire and Llŷn. Seasonality all year.

Bass/sea bass

This member of the perch family is one of the most sought after species by anglers and gourmets alike. Silver bellied and slate grey backed with a characteristic spiny dorsal fin, this hunter of the seas is caught off the Welsh coast (particularly Llŷn, Pembroke and Gower) from Spring until late Autumn. It has pure white flesh with a deep sweet flavour and medium texture. Wild bass weighing from 2–3 kilos are the best. Imported farmed fish from the Mediterranean weighing about 500g do not have the texture or flavour of the wild. The ubiquitous thin 'sea bass fillet' does not compare with a chunk from a larger wild fish. They can be caught all year though they spawn in April and May, the main season is May – October, 'from when the bracken sprouts until it turns brown'.

Cod

This popular fish is landed in great quantities but recently has joined the endangered list. In Wales it is more common in winter and anglers might catch some large fish. Green grey and hazelnut brown spotted with a white belly. It has firm textured white flaky flesh and is popular in the fish and chips market, though many top restaurants now serve it. 'If it commanded the price of salmon it would gain the culinary recognition it so rightly deserves' wrote Auguate Escoffier over a century ago. Seasonality all year, but caught locally September – March.

Hake

Hake was the main fish landed in west coast fishing ports, particularly Swansea and Milford Haven by deep water fleets. Iron grey and silver bellied with its elongated body, it can grow to two metres. Its white, soft flesh is very palatable and popular in European cuisine. Seasonality – all year. But little is landed in Wales now.

Pollack

This dark metallic green fish is similar to cod without the speckled markings, yet in no way has the culinary value. Soft insipid flesh can be seasoned or smoked to palatability but is definitely an inferior specie. It can be caught all year, all around the coast, particularly in rocky areas. Seasonality all year.

Whiting

This yellowish-bronze backed and silver bellied fish has soft and flaky flesh, used in Victorian times as food for invalids. In winter it can be caught in quantity by anglers. Seasonality all year.

Gurnard

(grey and yellow gurnard)
This armoured-headed and large-finned fish has been mainly used as bait for lobster fishing. It is landed by inshore trawlers, particularly in Pembrokeshire. The flesh is remarkably tasty and firm-textured and now gaining culinary recognition. Main season April – October.

Sea bream

This plump-bodied fish with a dark slate back and silver belly is caught by anglers in the Autumn off the coast of West Wales. Its firm flesh is similar to bass. Farmed fish from the Mediterranean are becoming increasingly popular on menus. Main season July – October.

Grey Mullet

This grey backed silver bellied fish lives mainly in estuaries where it grubs for algae and small invertebrates. The flesh is white and slightly oily, not dissimilar to bass and has become increasingly popular in recent years. It is frequently caught in quantity in waterways, particularly in Pembrokeshire. Main season May – October.

Red Mullet

This small pinky red fish was highly esteemed in Roman times and found in the Mediterranean and off Western coasts, particularly Pembroke and Gower. It is best cooked whole with its liver and hence known as 'the woodcock of the sea'. The highly flavoursome firm, flaky flesh has become popular in restaurants, usually cooked as fillets. Main season July – October.

Dover Sole

This is the most highly-prized of commercial fish, caught by inshore trawlers of the west coast of Wales. It hunts on rocky ground feeding on worms and shellfish. Its muscular, flexible body can tough head to tail and hence the muscles are powerful, giving firm wonderfully flavoursome meat. It is best cooked on the bone, plainly grilled. Main season May – November. They spawn from December – March when the flesh is very depleted and inferior.

Plaice

This very common flatfish has a greeny-brown back mottled with yellow to orange spots. It is landed in big quantities by inshore trawlers. Its medium firm flesh is delicately flavoured and usually served fried or grilled – often sold as fillets. They spawn in winter months when the flesh quality deteriorates. Main season May – November.

Flounder

This flatfish inhabits estuaries all around Wales and can live in fresh water for a time. Drab in appearance compared to plaice it nevertheless has firm, tasty flesh from eating worms and invertebrates. It is under-rated as a specie and hence very good value treated exactly as plaice or sole. Main season May – October.

Dab

This hazel nut-brown flatfish inhabits shallow bays, particularly Swansea, Carmarthen and Conwy. They can be caught in big numbers by inshore trawlers. The flesh is very firm and white with a sweet flavour. It is another under-rated specie. Main season May – October.

Turbot

One of the largest flatfish and can be landed by inshore boats in quantity – particularly in the Autumn and early Winter in Pembrokeshire, Llŷn and Gower. The mottled-brown blotchy skin with occasional bony tubercules makes it distinctive. The flesh is firm and flaky with a rich flavour and hence highly-prized. The heavy bones have glutinous qualities and so it is best cooked on the bone in cutlets. Main season August – December. It spawns in Spring when the flesh deteriorates.

Brill

Another large flatfish, this has medium-firm flesh, less glutinous than turbot but eats very well. Fawn-brown with tiny scales it is also best cooked in cutlets on the bone, though usually it is served in fillets. Main season August – December.

Lemon Sole

This plump rounded fish is smaller than brill with paler, blotchy skin and medium-firm flesh. It spawns later in Spring and is useful on menus when Dover Sole are out of condition. Main season May – December.

John Dory

This solitary hunter similar to a large, spiny angel fish swims upright and has distinctive 'thumb' marks either side of its green-gold body. It is caught by trawlers in increasing quantities but is not a major specie in the catch. The flesh is firm and succulent and highly-prized by top chefs. Main season May – October.

Skate

There are 14 different species of skate caught around British waters. All are of similar shape with wide 'wings' that are developed pectoral fins. Most are caught by inshore trawlers, particularly from Llŷn Peninsula, Pembrokeshire, Cardigan and Carmarthen bays. They are often caught from angling boats. Usually only the wings of the fish are landed; occasionally the jaw muscles called balls or knobs are cut out and sold. It is a cartilaginous fish and the flesh comes away from the flat sheet of bones easily once cooked. It has become far more popular in restaurants in recent years. The white flesh is very palatable when fresh, but takes on an unpleasant aroma of ammonia as it deteriorates. Seasonality all year.

Mackerel

The most northern member of the tuna family, mackerel are caught in great numbers when they shoal in the summer months all around the Welsh coast. Most are caught line fishing from small boats though some are netted by larger boats. Factory boats catch these in more northern waters literally by the shoal. The distinctive green-black-silver iridescences and scribble marks on their flanks mark their freshness. They are highly-prized and most delicious eaten very fresh. Main season June – September

Herring

At one time this was an important source of food for many parts of the coast of Europe. Great shoals migrated around the coast and the fishery at Nefyn was dependent on this specie. Now the only remaining fishery is on the River Cleddau in Milford Haven where herrings spawn in winter months. In the past, most were cured into kippers and bloaters in the curing houses at Milford Docks. Main season January – March.

Eel

The river eel lives most of its life in fresh water and can be found in all rivers and lakes in Wales. At sexual maturity they migrate down river and return to the Sargasso Sea to spawn and die. The flesh of eel is very rich and oily and is a great delicacy when smoked. Continental and far eastern cuisines consider the eel of high culinary value, though in Wales it is rarely used. The migrating season is October to December, though they can be caught all year.

The elver is the tiny baby eel just 3 – 5 cms long that return to our shores carried by the Gulf Stream. In the Spring they swim up river in great numbers accumulating in backwaters and at weirs into dense shoals where they can be caught. Large scoop nets are used particularly on the Wye and Severn rivers where elver fishing was an annual tradition. Now numbers have decreased drastically due to the use of pesticides on farms that has depleted the natural feed for eels.
Main season March – May.

Squid

There are dozens of species of squid that inhabit every ocean all of the cephalopod genus. They range in size from a few centimetres long to giant squid of over five metres that has tentacles extending to 10 metres. Many species are migratory, hunting for food and following shoals of other migratory fish such as mackerel, herring and sardine. Seasonal fisheries have developed in the Bristol Channel and in North Wales and these have great potential in the future. The white meat of the body and tentacles is highly-valued and commands an attractive price. Fresh squid is available in most fishmongers. Main season all year. Seasonality all year.

Cuttlefish

This cephalopod is a prehistoric hunter of the seas, similar to a squid but has a rigid white backbone. Similarly, they have a black ink resource that is ejected to confuse their prey. They are sometimes caught in lobster pots as the mesh makes attractive anchorage for their eggs. Fisheries have developed in other UK areas, catching cuttlefish with large ink-well style mesh pots. There could be potential to develop a similar fishery in parts of Welsh waters. Their meat is similar to squid but usually sold ready cleaned and frozen. Seasonality all year.

Salmon

A fresh run salmon that has just returned from the sea to its natal river is one of the most beautiful of all fish. Its sleek, smooth flanks glisten with purple lights concealing the amazing pinky-orange flesh that is most highly sought-after in top restaurants. Now farmed salmon has replaced most of the wild fish on menus. But the rivers of Wales from the Dee to the Wye still have runs of salmon through the season from Spring to Autumn. Main season April – August.

Sewin

This is a migratory version of the brown trout that feeds in local waters on sand eels and other small fish before returning to its natal river to spawn. The Teifi, Tywi, Rheidol and Dyfi are among the notable sewin rivers. The pink flesh of sewin is very succulent and appreciated by gourmets just as the sport of catching sewin is to anglers. Main season April – August.

Brown Trout

Wild brown trout inhabit most rivers and lakes of Wales and are fished by anglers yet rarely appear on menus of catering establishments. The best known lake for wild brown trout is Tal-y-Llyn near Machynlleth. Many reservoirs and lakes are stocked with rainbow trout *salmo gairdneri* both for sporting and commercial purposes. Trout farms in Pembroke and North Wales rear rainbow trout for the table in commercial quantities. Char are found in many of the lakes of Snowdonia thought to be remnants from the last Ice Age. Main season March – September.

Welsh meat

Meat Promotions Wales/Hybu Cig Cymru (HCC) was established in 2003 and is the strategic body for the promotion and development of red meat in Wales and the red meat industry in Wales. Its mission is to develop profitable and sustainable production and markets within and outside Wales for the benefit of all involved in the supply chain from pasture to plate.

Welsh beef

Cattle have been important to the Welsh economy since Roman times and were used as a medium of exchange. The traditional Welsh Black were known as 'Welsh Gold.' Beef and dairy products have always been a most important part of the traditional mixed farming practised, in most areas of Wales. The breeds that are found throughout Wales include Aberdeen Angus, Welsh Black, Hereford, Holstein, Charolais, Friesian, Red Poll, Jersey, Guernsey and Limousin. Welsh Black is a highly popular breed, but represents under 2% of the beef output from Wales.

Welsh lamb

The wild and rugged upland terrain that covers many areas of Wales from Snowdonia to the Brecon Beacons is suitable for the natural grazing of hardy sheep over the summer months. In the Autumn the flocks are brought onto lower pastures. There are over 20 million lambs bred annually and may be why Wales is synonymous with lamb. Natural upland grazing has long been recognised to produce meat of very fine quality and now Welsh lamb has a European Protected Designation of Origin status. The main season for Welsh lamb is from Spring to late Autumn, although many farms will now lamb twice a year in order to have continuity of supply.

Welsh lamb can be enjoyed throughout the year and gastronomic pleasure can be furthered by appreciating the provenance of lamb as the seasons unfold.

My categorisation of Welsh lamb covers all areas of Wales, but certain areas are renowned for specific qualities throughout the seasons.

Spring lamb – new season's lamb is highly sought after for its mild flavour and delicate texture. The flavour improves considerably when natural pastures that begin to flourish in May provide all the feed, and hence spring lamb is at its best in June and onwards. Some farms produce milk fed lambs for exclusive restaurants. This has a mild sweet flavour and supreme tenderness. Radnorshire lamb in June and July is a classic example of this style.

Pasture or hill lamb – lamb grazed in grass fields and on hills that have been replanted with grasses to replace natural heath and bracken. Rich pastures from plentiful spring rainfall produce superbly flavoured mild meat that is synonymous with spring lamb. This could be the classic style of Welsh lamb found in most areas. Elwy Valley lamb has been very successful in marketing lamb from the hilly areas of North Wales.

Moorland lamb – much of the uplands of Wales can be described as moorland and it was this lamb that excited the great international traveller George Borrow in the 1860s. The natural grazing consists of heather, grasses, moss and wild plants and induces a deep richness into the meat that is basically as organic as one could wish. Lamb from the Brecon Beacons, Black Mountains, Llanbrynmair and Llandegla moors are classic examples of this style that appears later in the season after summer grazing.

Mountain lamb – the higher pastures of Snowdonia, the Berwyns and Cambrian Mountains only flourish for a short period over the summer months. The animals have to forage for a mixture of heather, herbs, lichen, grasses, wild flowers and berries. This induces a deep herby complexity, almost gamey, flavour to the meat just as wild game birds acquire their flavour. The Snowdonia Mountain Sheep Society have been very successful in marketing their lamb to specialist markets.

Salt marsh lamb – vast areas of the coastline of Wales consist of sea marshes of alluvial material washed down from the mountains over the centuries. On spring tides these areas are prone to flooding. They have a rich diversity of plant life including a wide range of grasses, sea beet, purslane, samphire, mint and other herbs and wild flowering plants. True salt marsh lamb must be grazed on these areas and these must flood at least twice a year to qualify for salt marsh definition. Other coastal areas that flood naturally such as northern Llŷn qualify under this definition. It is only in recent years that this has been recognised to produce distinctively flavoured lamb and marketed as such. Hitherto, these lambs were absorbed into the general market and carried no premium.

Areas best known for salt marsh lamb are Weobly Castle farm, Llanrhidian, Gower, the salt marshes of Laugharne, the Dyfi, Mawddach and Glaslyn, plus Pontllyfni in Llŷn. However the season for true salt marsh lamb is limited to the Summer and Autumn when these areas have adequate growth of vegetation. There is a move to establish a genuine profile for salt marsh lamb from Wales.

Hogget lamb – that has lived through a Winter to the following Spring. This meat is mature and darker, with a rich flavour.

Wether – a sheep that has lived through two Winters.

Mutton – in recent years there has been a renaissance in interest in mutton for its culinary value. Sheep of three years or more qualify as mutton. Many are sold after their breeding life and meat quality can be poor. But farms that specialise graze the sheep for months to put on weight and good quality flesh that is very flavoursome. Elan Valley Mutton has become renowned for its traditional-style mutton.

Pigs – they are very much a part of mixed farming. Every smallholding and farm kept a few pigs for domestic consumption. Pigs that live naturally on free-range farms and forage for food develop a very fine flavour. The meat is darker than the pale pink of factory produced indoor pork farms. There is an increasing demand for quality pork, particularly from specific and rare breeds.

The more interesting breeds include Gloucester Old Spot, Middlewhite, Saddleback and Duroc. The total output of pigs from Wales is well under 100,000 carcasses a year and is very small within the Welsh meat industry. Some specialists and butchers produce fine cured hams and bacon.

Venison – Roe, fallow and red deer – There are herds of deer in several areas of Wales, mainly on the large estates where they were introduced centuries ago and have long been naturalised. The herds are culled by organised hunts to keep numbers in relation to the size of the estate. Big numbers can come from such estates as Margam in South Wales, Glan Usk and Brecon Court and others throughout Mid Wales and the Grosvenor and other estates in the north. They are sold by game dealers such as Vin Sullivan. The dark lean flesh is very popular in restaurants and is available from specialist butchers. Seasonality all year but fallow deer have a closed season from May – August.

Chicken – free-range chicken develops its muscles naturally from exercise and foraging for food. Those reared organically are generally slower growing than others and can take 12 – 14 weeks to reach maturity compared to 5 – 6 weeks for a battery chicken. The sign of quality is fully developed bones, particularly the breast bone which indicates good husbandry and natural development. The texture of good chicken meat should be close grained and firm and can be carved into slices. The leg meat will be distinctively darker with rich, full flavour.

Turkey – free-range turkey, similar to chicken, gains its quality through natural development and plenty of exercise. The quality of the food affects flavour and hence organically fed birds are more expensive than those on cheapest grain. The Norfolk Bronze turkey that is slow-growing and fine-flavoured is becoming increasingly popular on farms in Wales, particularly Pembrokeshire and on Rhug Estate.

Goose – free-range geese exercise naturally developing a deep breast with copious dark meat under a generous layer of fat. The rich flavour of goose is one of the finest of all meat and the natural fat keeps the meat moist and succulent during cooking. The first cull of the herd is at Michaelmas (September 25) when the birds are full sized but have not put on excessive fat. A Michaelmas goose makes a fine autumn feast. By Christmas the birds will have put on big layers of fat that makes it the richest meat of all. The fat is useful for cooking, particularly making pâtés and terrines and also for roasting vegetables, particularly potatoes and parsnips. Main season October – January.

Duck – the domestic white duck has much lighter flesh than goose, but if free-range and even organically fed it has a very fine flavour and generous succulent medium-dark meat. The black and white farmyard Muscovy duck has much darker meat closer in style to goose, but without the excessive fat. These birds can have supreme flavour without the richness of goose. Seasonal throughout most of year.

Pheasant – most pheasants are reared in incubators and fed in pens until being released into the wild at the start of, and throughout, the shooting season. Estates that allow the birds to naturalise benefit from far more challenging sport, and the quality of the meat when the birds forage naturally improves greatly. The mild gamey flavour of pheasant makes it the most popular game bird in retail shops and restaurants. In cold weather the birds can be hung for several days during which time the muscles break down and the texture and flavour of the meat improves considerably. Pheasants can be purchased from shoots and game dealers at a very reasonable price. Estates throughout Wales have organised shoots. Main season October 1 – January 31.

Partridge – the English Grey Legged Partridge is smaller than the French Red Legged but considered a superior bird. These are reared the same as pheasants for shoots. A partridge is a popular one-portion game bird in restaurants. Main season September 1 – February 11.

Grouse – the indigenous Red Grouse does breed in some upland areas of Wales, particularly on the Llanbrynmair moors, but numbers are limited. The elusive Black Grouse does inhabit some forest areas and have been seen in Coed y Brenin. Main season 12 August – December 10.

Woodcock – this small wild game bird migrates to the milder Welsh climate during the Autumn and Winter and is found throughout woodlands. Long beaked with beautiful brown camouflage, it is one of the most highly-prized game birds. Intensely flavoursome with dark flesh it is cooked intact with viscera using the beak as a skewer through the body. The flavour is incomparable but for its smaller cousin, the snipe. Main season September 1 – January 31.

Snipe – a small wild game bird that migrates to marshland throughout Wales during the Winter. It is similar to, and treated the same as woodcock. Main season August 12 – January 31. Both snipe and woodcock are available from game dealers.

Mallard – wigeon, teal. The mallard is the largest of the wild duck followed by wigeon and the tiny teal. Mallard are found extensively on inland and coastal waterways, whereas the migratory teal and wigeon inhabit sea marshes such as Llanrhidian in Gower and estuaries of the Dyfi, Mawddach and Glaslyn. They are rarely seen commercially. Mallard has firm dark flesh with a rich flavour and a slight covering of fat. Like pheasant, it is a two-portion bird and very popular in top restaurants. Main season September 1 – February 11.

Pigeon – the slate-blue woodpigeon is very common throughout farms and woodlands in Wales. Large flocks can devastate crops and hence are shot in big numbers on farms. The dark meat is very tasty, particularly the younger birds that feed voraciously on corn from the stubble fields after the harvest. In the Winter, when many will feed on ivy berries the flesh can become very strong and is best used in casseroles and pies. Seasonality all year.

Rabbit – wild rabbits have regained numbers after they were devastated by disease in the 1960s, but not to the same level. They have never regained their popularity as an inexpensive food, but many rural restaurants and pubs use them in casseroles. Available all year from game dealers.

Hare – though similar in appearance to a large rabbit, a hare is considered as game. These sporting roamers of the fields and uplands have close-textured dark flesh that is very rich and flavoursome. They are available from shoots and game dealers. Main season August 1 – February 28.

Vegetables

Most of these are available in farmers' markets where the quality, particularly if they are grown organically, can be far superior to mass-produced fertiliser-fed crops from large arable farms. The main season is noted if appropriate.

Asparagus – green lauris asparagus (as opposed to the continental white argenteuil) is now grown in many domestic gardens and by vegetable farms in Wales from Pembrokeshire to the Wirral. The scale is very small compared to Evesham and Norfolk in England, but several restaurants have secured local supplies. The short season is from April until mid June.

Jerusalem Artichoke – this root vegetable is similar to a knobbly potato and grown by small holdings and organic farms. Not to be confused with the continental Globe artichoke. Main season Winter – Spring.

Runner Bean – the most flavoursome variety of green bean is grown by small holdings and vegetable farms. Main season Summer – early Autumn.

Broad Bean – the tasty bean at the heart of british cooking is grown on a small scale by farms in Wales, particularly Monmouthshire. Main season late Spring – early Summer.

Purple Sprouting Broccoli – the tender shoots and heart of broccoli are one of the finest winter vegetables, often compared to asparagus. Main season winter and spring.

- **Beetroot** – the staple red root vegetable has been a stand-by in all domestic gardens. It is now becoming popular used as a vegetable and in salads. Main season Autumn – Winter.

- **Carrot** – look in farmers' markets for organically grown ones that have a far superior flavour – as with all the following vegetables.

- **Cauliflower** – this is now an important vegetable grown on farms in Gower, Pembrokeshire and Vale of Glamorgan in particular. Grown mainly for the supermarkets.

- **Spring Cabbage** – large green leaves are full flavoured and good with roasts. January King has purple edges to the tightly packed green leaves.

- **Calabrese** – green broccoli, now a very popular vegetable.

- **Celery** – use the tops in soups and stews, stalks with cheese. Celeriac (root celery) skin makes a wonderful soup, while the creamy white inside roasted or mashed, goes well with roast dinners and game.

- **Kale** – this cattle fodder is now becoming a trendy 'green' vegetable in Winter.

- **Leek** – the distinctive white and green leek is the mildest member of the onion family, both are very palatable used as a vegetable or in soups, stews and traditional Welsh cawl. Main season – Autumn Winter Spring

- **New potatoes** – Pembroke and Gower are noted for top quality, early new potatoes. Now the mass importation of new potatoes year-round has taken the high profits from growing these away. Main season May – August. Local new potatoes are the finest.

Spinach/Swiss chard – both are becoming popular, particularly in restaurants. The stalks of chard should be cooked separately then served with the lightly cooked green.

Turnip – the purple turnip is at the heart of many French bourgeois recipes.

Swede – cattle fodder to the French, the swede is popular cooked as a mash to accompany roasts.

Fruits

Soft fruits are grown on many farms across Wales often sold on a pick-your-own basis. Gooseberries, black and red currants, raspberries and strawberries are the most popular.

Orchard fruits are grown more widely in East Wales and on the borders. Apples and pears are grown for cider and perry. Plums and damsons are on a much smaller scale. Many farms have a few mature walnut trees that will yield a fair crop if harvested before the squirrels get them. Green walnuts can be harvested early Summer.

Salads

Tomato – available in farmers' markets from smallholders in their season from July – October, and from large industrial producers year round.

Cucumber and lettuce varieties Cos, Frisée, Oak leaf, Iceberg, Rocket – similar in availability to tomatoes.

Wild plants

Throughout the season from early Spring a host of plants, flowers and berries can be harvested. The most popular now are wild garlic or ramsoms in the Spring; elderflowers for wine and syrup; marsh samphire grows prolifically on salt marshes and in estuaries and creeks in Summer and Autumn (not to be confused with rock samphire that was popular in middle ages); elderberries and sloes are harvested in Autumn for wine and sloe gin. Whinberries are the most delicious wild fruit harvested on hills and moors in Summer and Autumn. They have a deep pungent berry flavour. Blackberries can be picked at the same time in hedgerows everywhere.

Wild mushrooms

Wild mushrooms appear in various places throughout Wales, in fields, woodlands and on cliffs. As with all wild fungi their appearance is sporadic and unpredictable, but species appear at certain times throughout the year. This outline guide to the main edible species covers seasonality and habitat.

St Georges mushroom

This appears in mid April until mid May and no other similar specie grows at this time of the year. These white-capped oatmeal-coloured gilled fungi grow in rings or clusters varying in size from 3 – 12 cms across the cap. Their mild, mealy flavour goes well with chicken, veal, egg dishes and fish.

Oyster mushroom

A brown-grey fan-shaped fungus with gills that grows on dead trees.

Summer mushrooms

Field mushrooms

Are found in fields and meadows in grass that's usually a darker colour to the surrounding, frequently in rings. They have white caps with pink gills that become darker as it matures until deep brown. The aroma is distinctive 'mushroom' and they are useful in a wide variety of dishes. Can be from 3 – 15 cms across the cap. They appear from late Spring to late Autumn, usually following warm, damp weather.

Chanterelle or girolle

This funnel-shaped orange fungi with stem and cap in one develops distinct gills and a concave cap as it grows. The aroma is sweet and fruity. The flavour is ripe and mellow, the texture is firm and juicy. It is particularly attractive with fish such as turbot, veal and poultry. They tend to grow in clusters in fields, on the edge and in woodland, appearing from early Summer until late Autumn. The size is from 2 – 4 cms across the funnel.

Summer and Autumn

Parasol mushroom

Large umbrella-shaped mushroom with white gills – take care not to confuse with the death cap *amanita phalloides*.

Cèpe, porcini or penny bun

The most highly-prized mushroom of all has a distinctive nut-brown domed cap (becoming flatter as it develops) with sponge-shaped oatmeal-to-off-yellow tubes, becoming darker as it grows. The bulbous off-white stem is distinctive. Its habitat is in oak and beech woods and in fields surrounding woods-appearing during, Summer through to early Winter. The cap can be from 3 – 20 cms across. Closed-cup less mature specimens have a sweet vegetal, almost asparagus taste that is attractive with light meat, the more mature ones have a very deep, earthy pungency that adds immense flavour to soups, stews, risotto and sauces. They can be cooked, bottled or frozen, or frequently they are dried and reconstituted later for use.

Autumn to Winter

Blewitt, Wood Blewitt

This striking looking fungi has distinctive violet to mauve gills and stem, a brown conical cap with a pungent, sweet mushroom aroma. They can grow up to 15 cms across the cap. They can be found on cliffs, fields and on the edge and inside woodlands from late Autumn to Winter even might be found in January in frosty weather. The rich flavour is perfect with all game, particularly pheasant and partridge.

Cultivated mushroom

These can be used in all recipes calling for mushrooms. Their flavour is enhanced by using other aromats such as shallots and garlic.

Bread

Welsh cakes – spiced currant cakes cooked on a griddle.

Bara – staple white bread best made from the buff coloured organic flour.

Bara gwenith – made from the freshly milled organic wholemeal flour.

Bara brith – literally speckled bread with currants, brown sugar and spice.

Cheese

Caws Celtica – hard ewes' milk cheese from West Wales.

Caws Cenarth Caerphilly – traditional Caerphilly, brie style Perl Wen and semi soft blue Perl Las

Gorwydd – real unpasteurised whole milk farmhouse Caerphilly with a natural rind a wonderfully earthy farm flavour and crumbly texture.

Llanboidy – farmhouse cheddar with a grassy flavour from mature pastures, and a slightly crumbly texture.

Caerfai – organic farm cheddar from the cliffs of St Davids where the sea spray gives a distinctive tang to the milk from the very green pasture.

Nant y Bwla – farmhouse Caerphilly from the edge of Carmarthen town. Made from cows' milk from the wonderful verdant pastures.

Cothi Valley – a large farm with a herd of goats feeding on totally natural pasture in the rolling countryside of the River Cothi. They make a range of styles from ripe soft fresh brie-style cheeses to firm-rinded cheddar with a full sharp-ripe flavour.

Mynydd Du – ewes' milk cheese from the sheep that graze on the vast natural pastures of the Black Mountains between Talgarth and Crickhowell. The firm style of cheese has a mature distinctive flavour and texture.

Teifi Farmhouse cheeses

– unpasteurised cows' milk is the backbone of the range of cheeses from this farm in

Ceredigion. Semi-soft pungent washed-rind Celtic Promise and the firm gouda-style Teifi both have great natural flavour.

Pant Mawr Farm – in the Preseli Mountains, makes a range of cheese from cows' and goats' milk from farms in the area. Brie-style Preseli has a creamy grassy flavour, Cerwyn (after the highest peak in the range) is a firmer, stronger style.

Pont Gâr – a modern cheesemaker producing quality commercial mini brie, blue and flavoured brie, plus the distinctive Llangloffan, originally from Castlemorris in north Pembrokeshire.

Kid Me Not – semi-soft goats' milk cheese to partner the goats' milk fudge made on the farm in the Cothi Valley.

Snowdonia Cheese Company – wax-wrapped mature cheddar and with many added flavours that are very popular in the retail market.

South Caernarfon Creameries – very high quality for a cheddar produced on a large scale.

Merlin – wax-wrapped hard cheese from goats' milk also comes in various flavours.

Cadog – mature cheddar from North Wales.

Laverbread, laver, bara lawr

If there is one truly Welsh speciality it is laverbread made from the seaweed *porphyra umbilicalis* that grows around the coast of Wales. The weed is unique in that it is just one cell in thickness and hence cooks to palatability more easily than other seaweeds. World wide it is by far the most important edible species. It is eaten in big quantity in the Far East, particularly Japan where it is made into Nori for sushi and other culinary presentations.

In Wales eating laver in Pembrokeshire was mentioned by Giraldis Cambrensis in the twelth century on his journey through Wales. It was documented in Cambrens Britannica in 1607.

The height of the industry was in the late nineteenth and twentieth century during the coal mining era. It was eaten as part of a cooked breakfast. Its health giving properties from high levels of iron and iodine combated thyroid problems inherent in the coal mining areas. It was consumed in such spa towns as Bath and sent to other mining areas in Derbyshire.

Laverbread is sold in markets throughout south Wales, particularly on the cockle stalls in Swansea Market. It is also produced in cans by The Welsh Barrow and by Parsons Pickles and sold in delicatessens and food stores.

Harvesting, cooking and serving

Laver can be gathered from rocky beaches at low tide. Its distinctive fine texture and shiny raven-black colour make it quite distinctive.

A few kilos can be gathered with ease. It has to be washed very thoroughly to rid of any grit, sand hoppers and other weed. It can then be boiled with a little water for several hours to make laverbread or used from raw in other ways. Laverbread takes its name from the Welsh bara lawr – bread or food from laver. It is traditionally made into small cakes by mixing with oatmeal and fried in bacon fat as part of breakfast. It is often simply warmed through in bacon fat. Cooks experimented with laver in the nineteenth century serving it with roast mutton in a sauce flavoured with Seville orange juice; adding it to a leek soup or to cawl; and serving it with fish. Many chefs are now experimenting with seaweed in dishes as it brings a natural vegetal flavour and texture to many dishes. It is equally adaptable in meat, seafood and vegetarian dishes. Some Welsh cheesemakers put laver into the cheese to give a variation of flavour (e.g. Llanboidy, Teifi Farmhouse, Nant y Bwla). It can be added to bread and biscuits (e.g Daffodil Cottage Laverbread Oatcakes), or into meat, fish and vegetarian pies (Harvie's Pies), or into pâté (Patchwork, Romy Cuisine).

Laver canapés

Use as Welsh caviar and serve on biscuits, toast, blinis with a variety of other flavours e.g. sour cream and chives; smoked fish pâté; taramasalata; fresh or smoked mussels, oysters, clams, cockles; smoked meats; cream cheese; hummus; antipasta vegetables and charcuterie.

Laver balls

Mix with oatmeal, sesame seeds, pumpkin seeds and seasoning until it form easily onto 2 – 3cm balls. Either bake in the oven or deep fry until crisp and serve with a slightly spicy dip. These can be made in advance and reheated prior to serving.

Laver sauces

Laver to a variety of sauces to accompany fish, meat and vegetarian dishes. E.g to a beurre blanc sauce; to a tomato and olive oil sauce to serve with fish or poultry; to a vinaigrette for a salad; to mayonnaise for a different sauce for fish; to a gravy for meat, particularly lamb; to a white sauce for ham; to a herb pesto sauce for pasta or a pizza topping.

Laver and eggs

Laver to scrambled eggs for a really different flavour; to an omelette to Spanish tortilla; to egg mayonnaise; to a wine sauce for poached eggs; add to a quiche mixture for Quiche Lorraine or a vegetarian quiche, particularly from leeks.

Laver batter / pancakes

Add some laver to the batter for a pancake, or to the batter for coating fried fish or vegetables; add to the French speciality socca, made from chick pea flour (gram flour) substituting laver for half the water. This can be made into large pancakes or small canapé size blinis for a cocktail party as above.

Laver crisps – using raw laver

When thoroughly washed, dry the weed by ringing in a cloth. Cut through a handful of weed into smaller pieces. Dust with flour and shake off excess using a sieve. Deep fry in small batches in oil at 170C for 2 – 3 minutes stirring several times to separate until crisp. Drain well of excess oil, season and serve as a canapé or a garnish for seafood dishes, a seafood platter, mixed grill or as a snack. Use different flour for variations – e.g. wholemeal flour; gram flour; semolina; or flour flavoured with spices such as paprika, turmeric; coriander; cayenne etc.

Recipes: sea

Flake together both white and dark crab meat and arrange in four shells. (page 158)

Gratin of shellfish

with laver

Use a large oval gratin dish, or individual gratin dishes or ramekins
300g laver, laverbread
300g freshly cooked cockles, mussels, clams (or a mixture of the three)
150 – 200g slightly stale bread or fresh breadcrumbs
2 large sprigs parsley
50g cold butter in small pieces
Seasoning

1. Heat grill or oven to 250C, 450F, gas mark 8.

2. Make breadcrumbs in a food processor. Add the parsley to chop well, then add butter and pound for a few seconds to make a gratin topping. Refrigerate until use.

3. Put laver into gratin dish or individuals.

4. Top with shellfish and then coat with breadcrumb mixture.

5. Put in oven or under grill and cook until heated through and the topping is golden and crisp.

6. Serve as a starter or a snack.

Variations:

7. Season the laver with tarragon vinegar, balsamic vinegar, soy or Worcester sauce, lemon or lime juice, sesame oil, herb infused oil.

8. In place of the shellfish use fresh fish cut in fingers or small pieces; use any trimmings or cold cooked fish; smoked fish such as cod, haddock, whiting; tinned tuna or salmon in flakes; salted fish such as cod that has been well soaked.

9. For a vegetarian dish use any combination of part cooked vegetables, particularly leeks in place of the fish.

One of the best ways to enjoy the bounty from the sea is a seafood soup. (pages 160–161)

Put opened oysters into a grill tray and top with Perl Las blue cheese. (page 155)

cockles

fresh oysters

Eaten raw are possibly the most perfect complete gastronomic experience

Open the oyster

The great Welsh oyster fisheries are now confined to the history books. However in the late seventeenth century the oyster fishery of Swansea Bay and the Bristol Channel was documented as the finest in Britain. In the 1870s over 180 oyster boats were registered with output reaching 50 million in some years. In the latter part of that century landings declined and by the 1930s the fishery has ceased. At its peak over 600 people in Mumbles were gainfully employed in the industry, and the staple food of many households was oysters. It is recorded that oysters were eaten in an omelette, fried with bacon and inserted into a beef steak then fried or grilled and called a 'carpetbag' steak.

Fresh oysters eaten raw are possibly the most perfect complete gastronomic experience. Lightly cooked they are very delicious and many consider these to be more palatable. The oyster now generally available is the Pacific Rock Oyster as opposed to the Native Oyster.

To open oysters use an oyster knife or a stout knife with a rigid blade. Secure the oyster cup shell down on a board held with a cloth and insert the knife at the hinge or the side of the shell and prize open, cutting through the adductor muscle to loosen it from the shell.

Alternatively put six oysters on a plate and cook in the microwave for 30 seconds (depending on power) or longer until the shells gape slightly so a knife can be easily inserted to cut the muscle. If serving raw simply cool in the fridge, or use straight away in any of the cooked dishes. Always serve oysters in the deep shell with as much of the natural juice as possible. Retain any excess juice for use in sauces or any dish. The juice has a delicious saline shellfish savour and complements fish, meat and vegetables. Shucked oysters in their juice will keep for two days in the refrigerator.

Oysters grilled with Perl Las

and oatmeal crust

12 oysters opened in the deep shell
50g Perl Las blue cheese (Caws Cenarth)
50g crème fraiche (Rachel's Organic)
4 oatmeal biscuits (Daffodil Cottage) pounded
   to crumbs

1. Heat grill.

2. Put oysters into a grill tray or earthenware dish. Top each with half a teaspoon of Perl Las and crème fraiche, then sprinkle generously with oatmeal crumbs.

3. Put under grill, not too close to heat to allow heat to cook the shellfish.

4. Grill for about 5 minutes until the crust is golden and the oysters hot through.

5. Serve with fresh lemon and Tabasco sauce if desired.

Oyster sauce

(sauce Prunier)

This simple oyster sauce named after the famous fish restaurants in London and Paris will go with any fish dish, a carpet bag steak, other grilled meat, poultry and vegetables. Its truly natural flavour comes from the oyster juices and the oysters are amazingly succulent.

8 oysters, opened and shucked in a bowl with
   all juice
40g butter
Juice half a small lemon
100ml single cream or crème fraiche.
Dash of Worcester sauce, or Tabasco sauce
Freshly milled white pepper.

1. Large egg yolk (or 2 small) from an organic free-range egg.

2. Melt the butter in a pan on a medium heat without colouring.

3. Add oysters, the juice (take care not to pour in the very bottom of the bowl where any tiny fragments of shell settle) and lemon.

4. Swirl the pan to mix. When the oysters begin to curl at the edges they are just beginning to cook through.

5. Mix the egg yolk and cream together and pour into sauce, stirring continually and the sauce will thicken.

6. Remove from heat and continue stirring, adding the Worcester or Tabasco sauce and pepper to taste. Serve immediately.

Other uses for oysters
Add some oysters and juice at last minute to a favourite pie recipe e.g. steak pie; fish pie, chicken and leek pie (Mumbles pie); mutton/lamb pie.
   Add oysters to an omelette, scrambled eggs, or fry lightly with bacon to make a truly wonderful breakfast.

crabs

Always look for a crab that is heavy for its size. The claw tips should be very black, not grey

Consider the crab

The brown crab is very common all around the Welsh coast. It can be caught on the rocks on a low spring tide where it can be located in 'crab holes' or natural shelters in the rock strata. The Gower coast is a particular area where many local people go to the rocks 'crabbing'. They are also caught in lobster pots as a bi-catch, and now some boats fish specifically for crab. Interestingly crabs prefer fresh bait, whereas the lobster is partial to old, mature, even smelly bait.

Most crab caught around the Welsh coast is exported. However it still represents the best value shellfish from the sea. It is highly appreciated as a speciality seafood and now very popular in restaurants. It is more difficult to prepare than lobster and hence less popular in busy kitchens.

The male crab is distinguished by its large claws, narrow tail and flat back shell. The female has a wide tail, an arched back and relatively smaller claws. The male (cock or bull) is best for the white meat from the claws; the female (hen or cow) has the better dark meat.

Crabs grow by the process of ecdysis, moulting their old shell to produce a larger soft shell that hardens in time. It can take several months for the crab to feed sufficiently to grow new muscle to fill the shell; hence some crabs can be 'watery' inside.

Buying crab

Always look for a crab that is heavy for its size. The claw tips should be very black, not grey. A certain amount of tube worm or barnacles on the shell indicates it is mature and likely to be full of meat.

To prepare crab

Crab is cooked by simmering in salted water for a few minutes. However they have to be killed before cooking, or they cast many of their legs and claws during cooking making them more difficult to present and prepare. They can be killed by stabbing with a skewer in the indentation under the tail, or by drowning in fresh water for a short time, during which all oxygen is exhausted from the water. Either way they should then be boiled immediately.

Cooking in a court bouillon greatly enhances the flavour of the shellfish. For two litres of water add 200g of mixed chopped onion, carrot and celery plus a sprig of parsley, bay and thyme, and salt (30g per litre) and pepper to taste.

Always put crab into boiling water. Surveys by the Fishmongers Company have endorsed this as the best way to cook crabs (and lobsters). Once that water returns to the boil the heat should be turned down to a minimal simmer for three minutes for small crabs and five minutes for large crabs and then turned off. The crabs should be left to cool in the water, or removed when hand hot if being served warm. Once cold they should be refrigerated either in or out of the water. The cooking water can be reserved for use in fish soups or as a stock for risotto or other dishes or sauces noting it is quite salty.

Dressed crab – removing the meat from the shell

Start by pulling apart the back shell from the body, working from the base of the legs where they meet the tail. Sometimes it is easier to twist a blunt knife between the tail and back shell to separate the two. Inside it will reveal the gills, or 'dead mans' fingers' which should be removed. They are not poisonous, but as gills on a fish they are unpalatable.

In the back shell just below the eyes is the mouth. This is attached to the stomach which must be removed. Press down on the mouth until it parts with a click, then pull out and the stomach will be attached. Discard this with the gills. All other meat is edible and tasty.

Remove the dark meat from the back shell using a spoon or a wide bladed table knife. The meat from hen crabs is usually firmer and milder so keep the two separate for different dishes. Also remove the lump of dark meat from between the base of the legs in the 'honeycomb' and put with the rest.

To extract all the succulent white meat from the claws, legs and body start by removing the claws and legs, pulling off the base knuckle joint of each to reveal the white meat of the honeycomb. Pick the meat from this base joint then separate each at the joints and group ready for picking. Move the thumb of the claw to help release the meat inside. The end two joints of the claw may require a tap with a weight, the back of a kitchen knife or a light hammer to separate.

Use a nut cracker to crack the base of the legs and the end joint of the claws, and other leg joints on larger crabs. The meat from the two base claw joints can be removed without cracking the shell. Use a crab pick, base of a teaspoon or narrow blunt knife. Crack the end claw using a weight as above. Remove all meat. Always examine carefully not to have any sinew or shell mixed in.

Remove the meat from the body or honeycomb with a pick carefully taking each compartment at a time. It is surprising how much meat can be extracted very easily and it is the most succulent of all. All the shells can be re-boiled in the cooking water to make a stock; an immense flavour can be extracted. Cook for 20 minutes, cool, drain juice and refrigerate until use. It will keep for three days, or can be frozen for later use. The white meat is flaky with a succulent texture. The claw meat can be kept in large pieces to give a varied texture to any preparation; its red-brown edge can be most attractive against the pure white of the flesh.

The brown or dark meat can vary considerably in strength and pungency. Generally the meat of the hen is milder and more attractive. It can be very firm and will even cut into slices, giving supreme texture to dishes. The green-brown meat of a cock might be too strong for some dishes, but is excellent in soups and sauces when its flavour can be blended with others.

Crab in shell

This can be presented with the dark and white meat separated, or mixed together either by lightly forking to keep the texture of each, or mashing to form a spread. The meat can be seasoned and mixed with a little mayonnaise and lemon juice. Either way it can then be presented with a salad and new potatoes as a starter or main course.

Grilled crab with Manzanilla

400g white crab
100g dark crab
4 cleaned crab shells, scallop shells or
    gratin dishes
100g beurre blanc sauce (or plain unsalted
    butter)
50ml Manzanilla Sherry
Pinch cayenne pepper or a dash Tabasco
    sauce

1. Heat grill or oven to 200C, 400F gas mark 6.

2. Flake together both white and dark crabmeat and arrange in four shells or dishes not more than 1½ cms deep.

3. Mix sherry and cayenne into the sauce (or melted butter) and drizzle over the crab.

4. Place under the grill for 2 – 3 minutes until golden on top and hot through.

5. Serve immediately.

Fresh crab

Quick crab soup

200g brown crab meat
50g onion chopped
2 cloves garlic crushed
25ml oil
100ml dry white wine
450g tin chopped tomatoes
250 ml fish or vegetable stock
1 teaspoon basil pesto

1. On a medium heat fry onion and garlic in oil until soft but not coloured. Add crab meat and cook for 2 minutes. Add wine, cook for a minute then add tomatoes and stock. Simmer for 5 minutes than mash or liquidize with the pesto Check seasoning and serve.

Crab risotto

100g shallots chopped
2 fat cloves garlic crushed and chopped
50ml oil
200g aborio rice
75ml Manzanilla sherry
500ml crab stock or vegetable stock
100g dark crab meat
100g white of leek chopped (optional)
100g white crab meat
Chopped fresh parsley
50ml tomato juice

1. Fry shallots and garlic in oil until just soft. Add rice and cook for 2 minutes to just take on a slight colour.

2. Add sherry and dark crab meat and cook for a minute, then begin to add the stock stirring regularly to mix well.

3. Add the leeks and more stock and cook until stock is absorbed adding more as required.

4. After 20 minutes the rice should be cooked, still slightly nutty with a little juice in the risotto.

5. Add the white meat, parsley and tomato juice, check seasoning and leave for 3 – 5 minutes to finish cooking off the heat.

6. Serve without cheese – as this would over power the flavour.

Gower seafood soup

Throughout Europe all coastal areas have a local seafood soup speciality made from the bi-products of the catch and the small fish and shellfish that do not have commercial value. Soupe de poisson, bisque, marmite du pecheur, bouillabaisse, Italian brodetto and Spanish zarzuela all have this similar theme. Over the generations they have become more sophisticated. Now many creative chefs in Britain make versions of a seafood soup.

The basic idea is to extract the flavour and gluten from the skin, bones and head of the fish and enhance this with crustaceans and aromats. Any fish can be used, the better ones being red mullet, cod, bass, turbot and salmon. The heads of prawns and other similar species contain the liver which imparts a deep concentrated flavour. The resulting soup is hearty and nourishing with many uses in catering and at home.

Fresh fish

Basic seafood soup

250g rock prawns in shell (available in all fishmongers)

500g or more fish bones, trimmings, skin and heads

4 cloves garlic crushed

50ml oil

Half a teaspoon each paprika, tumeric, coriander

250g chopped onion

150g chopped carrot and celery

1 red pepper, chopped

1 small head fennel, chopped (if available)

250ml white wine

Quarter of an orange

500g chopped tomatoes or 1 tin tomatoes

Sprig thyme or oregano and a few bay leaves

1 litre water (or stock)

Seasoning

Small bunch fresh coriander or basil (optional)

All weights are approximate and purely a guide.

1. De-head and shell the prawns. Reserve the meat for other use or garnish for the finished soup. On a medium heat fry the prawn shells in half the oil until they begin to colour. Add the garlic and spices and cook stirring frequently for a few minutes.

2. Stir in the onion, carrot, celery, fennel and pepper with the rest of the oil and cook until these are just beginning to soften.

3. Wash the fish trimmings (particularly heads) in cold water and drain.

4. Add on top of vegetables and stir fry for several minutes to mix the flavours partially cooking fish.

5. Add wine and cover for a minute, then add tomatoes, orange, herbs and water. Bring to a boil rapidly, test seasoning, stir well then turn to a simmer and cook for 30 – 40 minutes topping up liquid if necessary until the fish has broken down and all vegetables are cooked.

6. Allow to cool then remove orange peel and bay leaves.

7. Liquidize everything (but the heaviest bones from large fish) thoroughly until well puréed. Press through a sieve using a ladle in a circular motion to press down well.

8. The soup should be thick and slightly glutinous. Discard that remaining in the sieve, or give a quick second boiling with a little water and sieve again to extract the last of the flavour.

9. Test seasoning then re-heat to serve.

The peeled prawns, pieces of other fish, other shellfish such as cockles and mussels, brown crab meat can be added to give extra bulk and flavour.

This soup can be used as a base for fish sauces, as an addition to pasta dishes, risotto, seafood stews such as brodetto, zarzuela, bourride and bouillabaisse.

Other shellfish, particularly the carapace of a lobster chopped up, can be used in place of prawn shells to start the base of the soup or use heads of Dublin Bay prawns if available. Use the cooking water from crab or lobster in place of using plain water; a court bouillon from cooking salmon or other fish; some dark meat of crab, will all add extra flavour. There is virtually no limit to what fresh fish or shellfish can be added.

In France the soup is always served with croutons, garlic mayonnaise or rouilli (spicy red pepper sauce), and grated Gruyere cheese; Welsh Cheddar makes a good alternative.

Cured mackerel fillets

with pickled walnuts

8 very fresh mackerel fillets about 100g each

4 medium shallots

1 medium carrot and 1 stick celery, cut into julienne

250ml crisp white wine

2 dessertspoons freshly chopped parsley

50ml extra virgin olive oil

4 pickled walnuts in slices

2 dessertspoons of vinegar from pickled walnuts

1 teaspoon freshly ground spices (green peppercorns, coriander, cumin)

Anglesey sea salt

1. Lightly cook shallots, carrots and celery in a little oil. Add the wine and simmer for 5 minutes. Add half the spices and parsley, walnuts, vinegar, season with sea salt and keep warm.

2. Dust the fillets with the spices and fry in a medium hot pan for 20 seconds either side until just colouring, and transfer to an oblong dish in a neat row. Sprinkle with some parsley, olive oil and a little salt.

3. Spoon over the warm liquid to just cover the fillets. Top each with some of the vegetables and walnuts, then sprinkle remaining parsley and olive oil. Leave to cool then cover and refrigerate overnight.

4. Serve each fillet with a little dressed salad, the fish topped with the juices.

Pickled walnuts

flounders are flatfish
similar to plaice

Flounders and dabs

Flounders are flatfish similar to plaice, but drabber in appearance. They inhabit estuaries and bays and can be caught in large numbers. The flesh is firm textured and remarkably tasty. They are best over the summer and autumn. They spawn in winter and early spring when the flesh deteriorates.

Flounders are excellent grilled on the bone just as a Dover sole. It makes them far easier to eat if the frill bone is trimmed away right back to the main frame bone of the fish. This is called 'boxing' the fish and can be done with a strong kitchen scissors.

Hold the fish to the light looking at the white side and the line of muscles attached from the frill bones can be easily seen. Cut along thin line around the frill from head to tail, then what remains is very easy to eat. This is a very useful way to prepare all smaller flatfish such as plaice and dabs. Remove the head and tail. Use all trimmings for seafood soup as these muscles and bones contain much gluten. Notice that the fish is thicker on the dark side, the top, than the white underneath.

Flounders also cook very successfully as fillets or 'lasks' as called in West Wales. Their firm flesh holds together well and these are very easy to eat. A fishmonger will always fillet the fish for you.

Grilled whole flounder

Prepare fish as above. Heat grill and the grill tray with a little oil. I prefer not to flour the fish, simply place on hot tray dark skin down and turn over immediately, then put under grill the thick part towards the back of the grill, the hottest part, with tail at the front.

Do not turn the fish during cooking as the heat of the tray will cook the fish from underside which is the thinner side of the fish.

When the flesh just begins to split at the top it will be cooked through. Remove from grill using a flat fish slice pouring the cooking juice over. Serve with a beurre blanc, a sauce vierge, hollandaise or tartar.

Lasks of flounders

Dust the fillets either side with flour mixed with a little paprika shaking off any excess.

Fry a small onion or shallot thinly sliced in a tablespoon of oil, when just colouring push to the side of the pan then cook the fillets skin side down in the oil for 30 seconds then turn and cook for a further 30 seconds on the other side. Remove and keep warm while cooking the remaining fillets. Sprinkle the onion over the fillets and serve with wedges of lemon and homemade tartar sauce.

Wild Garlic

The mild herby aromatic vegetal savour of wild garlic gives it a wide range of uses for complementing fresh spring flavours – the sweetness of spring lamb; the purity of wild trout or fresh run sewin; the mild flavour of free-range spring chicken; the sapid freshness of newly grown spring vegetables. The fresh flavour makes it contrast with deeper tastes such as mutton and game. It can be added to many dishes to give a different twist of esters such as in mashed potato, pastry in sauces for meat, fish, pasta and vegetables.

Wild garlic is found in woodlands throughout Britain. It is in season from early March when it first breaks through the loam soil of the woodlands until it withers after flowering and the seed heads setting in July. It is best picked young and tender and used quickly as it wilts quickly. Store it in a cool place and chop immediately prior to use. The stems have much flavour so chop these finely and cook first adding the chopped or ripped leaves shortly before serving in a sauce.

Add wild garlic in this way to a beurre blanc sauce for fish. Add to a leek and potato soup for a real depth of flavour.

Make a pesto sauce by pounding the leaves and stems with nuts (walnuts or hazel) adding grated cheese by hand at the end. Use mature cheddar, Cheshire, pecorino or parmesan.

Add to a nut crust by mixing with the breadcrumbs and pounded nuts, butter, or oil and use to coat fish or meat, vegetables, as a topping for mashed potatoes or vegetables, fish pie, cassoulet or crumble. It can be used as an addition to stuffing for poultry and game.

Wild garlic vinaigrette – chop or pound in a food processor and add mustard diluted with a little wine vinegar and water, oil and seasoning. Serve this with salads and vegetables. Add some tomato coulis to make a sauce 'vierge' to accompany grilled fish, poultry and light meats, or to mix with pasta.

Wild garlic butter – chop by hand or pound in food processor and add softened butter and oil in equal quantity to make a light butter that will remain soft in the fridge or can be frozen for later use for up to three months. This can be used for garlic bread, a topping for vegetables, grilled meats and fish, snails, mussels, cockles, clams, prawns and lobster.

Wild garlic can be used with other spring vegetables and leaves such as young hawthorn, dandelion leaves, asparagus, broccoli and new potatoes.

Ceiriog trout or sewin fillets

with wild garlic butter sauce

4 Ceriog trout or sewin fillets about 200g each
2 medium shallots
1 medium carrot and 1 stick of celery, chopped
350ml dry white wine
Water
2 dessertspoons of freshly chopped parsley
Sea salt and pepper
200g freshly picked young wild garlic leaves
150g lightly salted butter
Juice of half a lemon
Dash of Tabasco sauce

1. Preparation and cooking time 30 to 40 minutes, serve hot.

2. Finely chop shallots and put half in a stainless or enamel pan with 200 ml of the wine. Bring to a simmer and cook slowly for 20 minutes to reduce to a quarter.

3. Remove the stalks from the garlic, reserve a few leaves for presentation and roughly chop the remainder and add to the shallots. Cook for 2 to 3 minutes. Then, over a medium heat add the butter in small pieces whisking continually with a balloon whisk until all has been absorbed and the sauce has a flowing creamy consistency. Add the lemon juice and Tabasco. Cover and set aside to keep warm.

4. In a pan large enough to take the four fillets make a court bouillon by combining the remaining shallot with garlic stalks, carrot and celery, remaining wine, water, sea salt and pepper to taste. Simmer for 5 minutes then carefully place in the trout fillets to just cover completely. Cook very gently barely to a simmer and turn off heat, not allowing fish to be in the water for more than 2 – 3 minutes.

5. Using a fish slice lift each fillet and place on the centre of four large plates, pour the sauce over the centre of the fish and around each plate. Decorate with garlic leaves. Serve with new potatoes and spring greens.

Recipes: land

Walnuts

Chestnuts are easy to prepare. (page 173)

Walnut trees are quite common throughout Wales, particularly on the large estates and farms. Green walnuts can be made into pickled walnuts, a quintessentially British speciality. These are usually served with cold poultry at Christmas, but they have a broad and exciting range of culinary applications.

Walnuts have to be picked green to be suitable for pickling. It has to be before the shell begins to form. After St Swithin's Day, July 15, they are usually too far developed. They need to be of reasonable size so the kernels have begun to develop, so pick them as early as possible.

Test each by inserting a skewer close to the stalk; if there is a resistance the shells have begun to form and it is too late.

As soon as they are gathered they should be pricked twice with a silver or wooden pick and immediately put into brine for seven days. This stops the shells from continuing to form even after they have been harvested. Remove from brine and dry in a warm sunny place – on a paper lined tray, turning them frequently until they are totally black.

Pack these into jars and cover them with pickling vinegar diluted with 25% water. Seal jars and leave for three months to mature.

The pickled walnuts should have a deep colour and inside a slightly creamy soft nutty texture. These and the juice of the pickled walnuts can be used in a variety of hot and cold sauces, and in casseroles and with cured meats and fish.

Pheasant, like other poultry, can be roasted, stuffed, pan-fried or used in a casserole. (page 172)

Welsh beef can also be enjoyed 'carpetbag-style' with oysters. (page 178)

Green walnuts

Terrine of wild rabbit, pork and wild mushrooms

with pickled walnut vinaigrette

Ingredients

1 wild rabbit, cut into 8 – 10 pieces
1 pig's trotter
200g shallots, chopped roughly
100g carrots, in 1 cm cubes
100g celery, in 1 cm slices
4 cloves garlic, crushed and chopped
4 sprigs each fresh thyme, parsley and bay
50 cl dry white wine such as Riesling
Seasoning – Anglesey sea salt and black
   pepper
1 teaspoon green peppercorns
500ml chicken or light game stock
250g wild mushrooms
6 large sprigs fresh parsley
Pickled walnuts and vinaigrette made in
   advance (see page 167)

1. Heat oven to gas mark 6, 200C, 400F.

2. Ensure all hairs are removed from the trotter. Put trotter into a large casserole and lightly oil and cook for 60 minutes in the oven turning a few times to crisp.

3. Lightly oil the rabbit pieces and put around the trotter and cook for 20 minutes to barely colour, then add the vegetables distributing them evenly around the meat. Cook for 20 minutes, then add the seasoning wine and herbs and enough stock just to cover. Stir carefully with a wooden spoon to ensure no meat is sticking to the pan.

4. Put lid on casserole and cook for a further 20 minutes. Check it is simmering then lower the heat to 110C and cook for 3 hours, checking a few times topping up the stock if necessary. Check that the meat is very tender and the skin of the pork is very soft. Remove from the heat.

5. Meanwhile clean and slice the mushrooms and cook in a little oil for 5 minutes, then add to the casserole when taken from the oven, mixing into the juices.

6. Line one or two pâté terrines with cling film, Leave a generous amount hanging over the sides.

7. When cool and easy to handle carefully remove pork trotter and pieces of rabbit and place onto a shallow tray.

8. Remove the meat from the bone keeping in as large pieces as possible. Remove bones from trotter reserving all the skin and meat and jelly. Slice skin into strips and line the bottom on the terrine. Chop the parsley.

9. Fill the terrine with the meat, vegetables, mushrooms distributing evenly with largest chunks of meat in the centre. Sprinkle parsley liberally as the terrine is filled, adding spoons of the juice to keep it very moist. Use all the vegetables, meat and juices. Top the terrine with lots of parsley then fold over the cling film. When totally cool place in the refrigerator for 24 hours minimum.

10. Remove the terrine from the dish by placing in hot water three-quarters of the way up the sides of the terrine for a few seconds until it lifts out easily on the cling film. Put on a serving plate and refrigerate until ready to serve. Use a very sharp knife and slice into pieces about 1 cm thick or more of desired. Serve with chopped pickled walnuts and some of the vinaigrette.

Woodcock dressed on game toast

with bread sauce and elder gravy

Ingredients

4 woodcock whole, plucked, un-drawn
    with heads on
8 slices organic white bread
2 shallots
6 cloves
250ml milk
250ml elderberry wine
1 head elderberries
Seasoning
25g butter

1. Heat oven to gas mark 6, 200C, 400F

2. Use the beak of the woodcock as a skewer and push through the base of the legs right through the body to the other side, the neck remaining attached. Lightly oil and put into roasting tray with one shallot finely chopped.

3. Stud other shallot with the cloves and put into pan with milk and simmer very gently for 20 minutes to infuse.

4. Use a cup to make four round pieces of bread, then make the remainder into breadcrumbs in a food processor or with a cheese grater.

5. Roast woodcock in oven for 15 to 20 minutes, seasoning and basting after 10 minutes. Return to oven until they are golden and cooked through.

6. Pour off all fat onto the rounds of bread and put then on an oven tray and put in oven for 5 minutes to crisp slightly.

7. Put woodcock into a warm serving dish, lightly cover with foil and keep warm. Add wine to roasting tray with the juices from woodcock and set on a medium heat to deglaze, mixing well. Reduce by a third, then add the elderberries and butter swirling pan to make a glossy sauce.

8. Remove shallot from milk, add sufficient breadcrumbs to make a flowing thick sauce, stirring constantly over a low heat.

9. Put the woodcock onto the toast in the centre of four warm plates, spoon elderberry sauce over each, and spoon some bread sauce on the side. The entrails and liver of the woodcock are great delicacies scooped out and squashed into the toast.

put in oven for 5 minutes to

crisp slightly

swirl the pan to make a
glossy sauce

Pigeon from the stubble fields
braised with elderberries

In summer after the corn fields have been harvested there is still much grain left on the stubble fields on which pigeons feed voraciously. This gives the flesh a supreme mild flavour. It is quite different from the strong flavour from eating ivy berries in the winter. Young pigeons usually still have some of their fledgling buff fluff around the neck and these make the best eating.

Ingredients

Elderberries are very plentiful at this time
  of the year.
12 breasts from young pigeon from summer
  corn fields
200g shallots finely chopped
4 cloves garlic crushed and finely chopped
250g fruity red wine
25g butter 25ml oil
4 heads fresh elderberries

1. Fry the shallots and garlic in oil until just soft. Cut each breast into two or three diagonal slices, place on the shallots and cook to sear quickly and then turn to colour on the other side. Season with sea salt and pepper. Remove meat and keep warm.

2. Add wine to pan and mix all the shallot and garlic into the wine and cook for 10 minutes to reduce by half. Add the stock and cook to reduce and begin to thicken naturally.

3. Using a fork remove the berries from the stems and add to the shallot sauce together with the butter, swirling pan to make a glossy sauce.

4. Add the pigeon breasts and any juices, mixing in carefully to coat meat quickly but not to cook further. Check seasoning.

5. Arrange meat and sauce onto four plates and serve with noodles, rice or traditional vegetables.

pheasant

can be purchased 'oven ready' from game dealers and in local markets and farmers markets

Throughout Wales on all estates pheasants have long been bred for sport. Now there are many wild birds that live naturally; but the majority are those bred and released into the wild. Fed on grain, then with naturally foraged food, pheasant has delicious meat with a very natural wild taste. Hanging the birds in a cool airy place or cold room allows them to develop even further flavour and texture.

In season pheasants can be purchased 'oven ready' at a very reasonable price from game dealers and in local markets and farmers' markets. At times they are even cheaper than a chicken in a supermarket, and hence represent superb value. They are even cheaper if bought in feather and they are very easy to prepare, though it is not for the faint hearted.

Start by removing the tendons from the legs, something no game dealers do. This makes the delicious drum stick meat very accessible. Break the leg between the bottom joint and the spur by cracking on the edge of a chopping board. Put the broken joint over a hook on the back of a door, hold the foot with one hand and pull down on the leg with the other. The tendons come out attached to the claws very easily.

Put the bird breast up on a board and take a few feathers from the firm breast bone to reveal some skin. Cut a small incision in the skin and using both hands tear the skin with feathers attached to reveal both breasts. Then peel it back over each leg and cut with a secateur or strong scissors through the bottom joint. Push the legs outwards to break from the base joint into the body. Cut each leg away.

Slide a sharp knife either side of the beast bone cutting as close as possible to remove the meat in single pieces. Lift the breast bone to reveal the liver and pull away and reserve for pâté of stuffing.

The yield is two breasts and two legs, making two very good portions.

Similarly the pheasant can be totally skinned whole in this way. It is then ideal for roasting wrapped in thinly sliced fat streaky bacon.

All other birds can be prepared in this way, particularly pigeon.

Mutton with bitter ale casserole

with chestnut dumplings.

Ingredients

1 kilo mutton, in 2 – 3 cm cubes
500g onions, in thick slices
250g turnips, in 1 – 2 cm cubes
100g celeriac (or celery) in 1 – 2cm pieces
4 cloves garlic, crushed and chopped
1 teaspoon mixed freshly ground white pepper,
    coriander and all spice
1 litre dark ale
Large sprig thyme and rosemary
100ml tomato juice
2 teaspoons mustard powder
Seasoning

Dumplings:

100g cooked, peeled chestnuts
50g vegetarian suet
Warm water
1 egg yolk
Seasoning

1. In a large casserole fry meat in a little oil
until colouring lightly.

2. Add vegetables, garlic and cook on a medium
brisk heat, cover and cook for 5 minutes
stirring frequently. Season with salt and the
mixed spices halfway through.

3. Add the ale to cover the herbs, bring to
a simmer and cook slowly for 2 hours until
tender, topping up the ale if necessary.

4 . Pound the chestnuts in a bowl, add the
suet, a little water to moisten and the egg yolk,
season and mix well. Form into egg shapes
using two teaspoons and drop into simmering
water for 1 to 2 minutes, drain and add
dumplings evenly to the casserole.

5. Dilute mustard with water or remaining beer,
mixing to a cream like consistency and add to
the casserole with tomato juice to completely
cover the meat and dumplings, mixing
carefully.

6. Cook over a low heat or in the oven on Gas
mark 2 for 30 to 40 minutes until the meat is
tender and the dumplings soft and slightly
fluffy. Check seasoning and serve with mashed
potatoes or rice, and a green vegetable.

Chestnuts

Chestnuts can be gathered in many woodland areas in the Autumn. Sometimes it is difficult to find large ones, but they are quite easy to prepare. Prick each one with a needle or skewer but for one or two. Cook these in simmering lightly salted water until the ones not pricked burst. This indicated all are ready and can be removed from heat. Remove the shells when still warm and use within a few days, storing them in the refrigerator. They can be bought tinned or vacuum packed usually produced in France.

stuffed breast and ale braised

leg of wild pheasant

Ingredients

2 pheasants prepared as per page 171
100g chicken liver pâté
8 small shallots
2 medium leeks
1 small carrot, cut in batons
1 litre bitter ale
200g chopped onion, carrot and celery
4 large sprigs fresh coriander
Oil and seasoning
25g butter

1. Breasts will make a dish or two legs a serving for one.

2. In the casserole fry the onion, carrot and celery to colour slightly then add the legs and shallots and cook either side for 5 to 10 minutes. Then add half the ale, the stalks of the coriander and simmer gently for an hour until the meat is tender. Add a little stock as necessary to keep moist.

3. Chop the coriander leaves finely and mix into the pâté, and check seasoning.

4. Place breasts of pheasant on a board, skin side down, and make an incision underneath the fillet into the thickest part of the breast to form a neat pocket in each. Using a round knife or spoon stuff the pocket with pâté. Spread evenly inside the breast. Fold the fillet back over to look neat.

5. Use the frying pan with lid. Cook the breasts on a medium heat in a little oil, smooth side down. Cover the pan so it will cook the meat through without turning or this will mis-shape the breasts.

6. Add the shallots and dust the breasts with seasoning and a little coriander, and cook until the meat has firmed up and is evenly coloured.

7. Put breasts onto a serving platter and top with the shallots. Keep warm.

8. Pour off the fat and add the remaining ale, swirling to take up all the caramelised bits. When reduced to half add the butter to make a small amount of glossy glaze. Pour over breasts.

Mint jelly

Ingredients

A generous handful tender mint leaves
Juice 1 lemon
25g sugar
50ml dry white wine
1 pack gelatine powder dissolved with
50ml water

1. Chop the mint very finely and immediately add to the lemon, sugar and wine in the pan.

2. Heat through very gently and simmer for 5 minutes. Remove from heat and add diluted gelatine, stir well and pour into a warm storage jar/s, close with lids and allow to cool.

Mint sauce – excellent mint sauce is available from the Welsh Mustard Company.

chop the mint very finely

Fresh mint

slow roast stuffed shoulder

of lamb with mint jelly

Ingredients

1 shoulder of lamb, complete with neck fillet
100g minced lamb
100g each chopped onions, carrots, celery
6 cloves garlic, crushed
Large bunch fresh mint
Seasoning
200ml dry cider
100ml reduced stock
50ml tomato pulp
2 teaspoons mustard

1. In a large casserole fry meat in a little oil until colouring lightly.

2. Ask your butcher to remove bone from shoulder by tunnel boning to form a neat pocket in the joint; then to chop bones into six pieces.

3. Lightly oil bones and put into roasting tray with vegetables and cook in oven for 15 minutes.

4. Remove tender leaves from the mint and reserve for the jelly. Add the stalks to the roasting tray.

5. Flatten out the shoulder so all the fat is uppermost, score the fattier areas.

6. Season the mince very well, adding some chopped herbs if available. Put into the pocket of the meat, pressing down well so it spreads within the pocket evenly. Close the end with a thin skewer, do not tie with string as the muscles will form to their natural shape during cooking.

7. Lightly oil and place fat up onto the vegetables and bones, and cook in the over for 30 minutes until fat is golden and crisp.

8. Remove from oven and baste meat well seasoning generously. Reduce heat to gas mark quarter, 95C, 210F, and cook for 3 hours, basting a few times.

9. Carefully remove meat to a serving dish and lightly cover with foil and leave in the oven turned to minimum with door propped open slightly for the meat to set for 30 minutes.

10. Pour off the excess fat from the roasting tray.

11. Add the cider and stock to the vegetables in the roasting tray, and cook on the hob on a medium heat to reduce. Remove bones and mint stalks (and use to make a stock for later use), add tomato pulp and mustard diluted with a little water or wine. For a thicker sauce liquidize the juice and vegetables.

12. When the meat is well set pour any juices into the sauce and carve into thick slices as the shape directs.

13. Serve with the sauce, lashings of mint jelly and hot new or baked potatoes.
Cook on medium heat to reduce.

lambs' sweetbreads

Young lambs, just as calves have large thyroid glands called 'ris' in French and sweetbreads in English. As the animal grows these glands decrease in size. They are very highly prized in French cuisine, virtually ignored in Britain. Any butcher will supply these in the Spring and early Summer. They are very easy to prepare and make a delicious mildly flavoured range of dishes. They should not be confused with the testicles that are sometimes sold a little later in the season. These do not have the nutty texture or mild spring meat flavour of the 'ris' or sweetbreads.

spring lambs' sweetbreads

with St George's Mushrooms

Ingredients

500g lambs sweetbreads
100g shallots chopped
200g mushrooms, cleaned and sliced
25ml oil
25g butter
50ml dry sherry or dry white wine
1 tablespoon freshly chopped mint
2 teaspoons Dijon mustard
100ml tomato juice or passata

1. Wash trim and dry sweetbreads and rip or cut into walnut sized pieces. Fry half shallots in a little oil and butter until soft and add some sweetbreads and stir fry briskly until they firm up. Season and keep warm. Cook all and keep warm.

2. Cook remaining shallots with mushrooms until rendered down and tender.

3. Return sweetbreads to pan and mix together over a brisk heat.

4. Add sherry and mint, cover and cook for a few minutes for flavours to mix.

5. Mix the tomato and mustard until smooth, and add to the pan mixing well to form an even sauce.

6. Serve in ramekins as a starter for four or with rice for a main course for two.

Lambs' liver

with elderberry sauce

Ingredients

400g fresh lambs' liver
4 shallots
4 heads fresh elderberries
100ml elderberry wine
200ml lamb stock
2 young leeks, trimmed, washed
25g butter
Seasoning
2 sprigs fresh mint

1. Cut liver into slices about 1 cm thick. Chop the shallots and fry in a little oil until colouring then fry liver with shallots quickly for 1 to 2 minutes either side. Season well, remove and keep warm retaining shallots any juices in the pan.

2. Add wine and reduce quickly to about half then add stock and cook down quickly, season and add elderberries and cook for 2 to 3 minutes.

3. Check seasoning, chop and add mint.

4. Cut leeks into strips and cook quickly in butter in a pan or microwave until just soft.

5. Put leeks in the centre of four warm plates, top with liver and pour sauce over and around the liver.

season with coarse ground black pepper and sprinkle with

shallots

rump of beef

'Carpetbag steak'

Ingredients

4 thick rump steaks about 250 – 300g each
2 shallots finely chopped
8 oysters for the steak
Freshly milled pepper and Anglesey sea salt
8 oysters for the top

1. Put steaks onto a board and make an incision into each to form a pocket to take the oysters.

2. Push two oysters into each steak.

3. Lightly oil each side of the steaks.

4. Season with freshly milled coarsely ground black pepper and sprinkle with shallots.

5. Heat pan on a medium flame and put steaks in with shallots to the pan.

6. Cook for about 2 minutes without moving the meat.

7. Use a fish slice and carefully turn over each steak.

8. Season with sea salt and cook for a further minute.

9. For very rare steaks remove and keep warm.

10. For rare cook a further minute (depending on thickness).

11. When beads of pink juice appear on top of the steak they are medium rare.

12. Cook a little longer for medium. Keep steaks warm, but do not allow to cook further.

13. Serve each topped with two oysters and the sauce.

Fillet steak may be used if very tender meat is preferred.

Welsh lamb braised in ale

with penny buns (cèpes)

Ingredients

1 kilo diced lamb
500g shallots
200g carrots
8 cloves garlic, peeled
2 sprigs thyme
Seasoning
1 litre real ale
250g trimmed penny bun mushrooms (cèpes)
25g butter 25ml oil
50ml cream
Fresh parsley

Note any variety of wild or field mushroom can be used (e.g. chanterelles, blewitts) or use cultivated mushrooms.

1. Heat casserole on hob with a little oil, roughly dice shallots and cook slowly until beginning to soften.

2. Heat frying pan with oil and quickly fry the lamb in small batches to seal to golden, season and add to casserole.

3. Halve garlic and cut carrots into batons and fry in pan and add to casserole with thyme and ale to cover. Bring to a simmer, cover and cook slowly for 45 minutes.

4. Remove lid and cook further to allow juices to reduce but not dry out cooking until the meat is tender.

5. Cut penny buns (cèpes) into thick pieces and fry in the oil and butter for 10 minutes until soft. Add the cream and heat through well. Season well and add lots of chopped parsley

6. Serve the lamb onto four large soup plates and top with the mushrooms.

Fresh carrots

Recipes: puddings

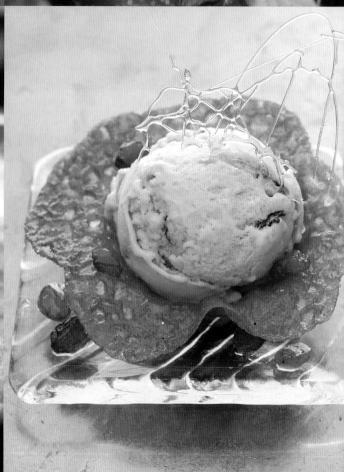

Soft fruits can be bought or foraged from the countryside. Use a mix of berries and other soft fruits in this Gratin of Summer Fruits.

Gratin of summer fruits

with elderflower, whinberry sorbet

500g mixed summer berries washed whinberries, wild strawberries, raspberries, blackberries etc
1 egg yolk
50g caster sugar
150ml white wine
25ml elderflower syrup
4 small balls (golf ball size) whinberry sorbet

1. Arrange fruit in four gratin dishes or on 4 small plates

2. In a large glass or stainless bowl whisk the egg yolk with the sugar very thoroughly until the mixture is thick and flowing from the whisk.

3. Add the wine and syrup and continue to whisk for 5 minutes.

4. Put the bowl into a larger bowl or pan of hot water and continue to whisk until the mixture becomes light and fluffy and has a thick but flowing texture.

5. Heat the grill to full. Put the gratin dishes onto one grill tray, top with the sauce to completely cover the fruit. Put under the grill and watch continually as it burns very easily. Cook for 20 – 30 seconds until the top of the sauce is golden brown. Remove and serve immediately, with the sorbet in a small dish on the side.

Elderflower fritters are best eaten with fingers. (page 182)

Bara Brith Ice Cream from Plas Farm Denbigh Farmhouse. (page 44)

To make sorbet
500g fresh whinberries
250g sugar
500ml fruity red wine

1. Put all into a saucepan and bring to a simmer, stirring regularly until the sugar has dissolved. Test for sweetness, adding more sugar if necessary.

2. Allow to cool then liquidise, and press through a sieve using a round ladle. Chill the purée then make into sorbet a sorbetier until a fine, dark sorbet has formed. It can be made in a deep freeze by pouring the puree into a shallow tray, place in freezer, and stir every 5 minutes until all has frozen.

3. Transfer into a plastic tub to keep in the freezer.

Whinberry

Summer pudding

1 kilo whinberries (or a combination of
    wild berries)
200ml dry white wine
200g unrefined caster sugar
12 slices day old organic white bread about
    1cm thick, crusts removed
few sprigs fresh wild mint

1. Reserve a tablespoon of berries and cook
the rest on a moderate heat in a heavy pan
with wine and sugar until the sugar has
dissolved and the fruit is soft. Snip a few
leaves of wild mint into the fruit and stir in.

2. Line a pudding basin or ramekins with
the bread, spoon in the berries and juice,
reserving a few tablespoons. Line the top
with bread and put a plate to fit just inside
the rim of the bowl, top with a weight and
refrigerate for at least 8 hours.

3. Take from fridge and remove plate. Place
a larger plate over the bowl and carefully
invert for the pudding set onto the plate. Use
the juice to colour the bread evenly. Top with
reserved berries and sprigs of mint.

4. Serve with organic clotted cream or
crème fraiche.

Elderflower fritters

with elderflower syrup

10 large heads freshly picked elderflower
1 large free-range organic egg
50g sifted organic white plain flour
75ml fresh whole milk
500ml sunflower or vegetable oil
Icing sugar (optional)

1. Make batter by separating egg and
whisking the yolk with the flour and milk
until very smooth. When ready to use, whisk
the white of the egg until very light and
frothy, and fold gently into the batter.

2. Snip large florets from the elderflower
heads, leaving a piece of stalk onto each.

3. Heat oil in a pan until hot. Dip a flower into
batter and test oil is hot enough. The flower
should sizzle and rise to surface almost
immediately. Dip each flower into batter and
drop into oil, and cook for about 30 – 60
seconds until just golden and crisp.

Dust with a little icing sugar for a sweeter
flavour.

4. Arrange on a large warm platter, drizzle
to the elder syrup and serve. Best eaten with
fingers!

Elderflower syrup (to be made before)
10 large heads freshly picked elderflower
500ml inexpensive white wine
100g sugar
Juice 1 large lemon

1. Snip the elder flowers from the stalks and
steep in the wine for 24 hours. Put into a pan
and bring to a simmer. Add sugar and lemon
and cook for 20 minutes.

2. Strain through a sieve and allow to cool.
More sugar can be added if a heavier syrup
is preferred. Leave to cool, bottle and store
in refrigerator.

Welsh honey, lemon and passion fruit tart

with blackberry sauce

225g plain flour
400g shortcrust pastry
125ml double cream
200g caster sugar
6 tablespoons honey
4 eggs
Rind and juice of 2 large lemons
Pulp and juice from 3 passion fruit
250g fresh blackberries
50ml brandy (optional)

1 Heat oven to gas mark 4, 160C, 320F

2. Roll pastry to fit tin neatly, line with foil and beans and bake for 15 minutes. Remove beans and foil and bake for a further 15 minutes, remove from oven and cool.

3. Whisk cream, 100g sugar, eggs, passion fruit, lemon rind & juice together with honey, pour filling into pastry case, bake in oven for about 20mins or until just set. Leave to cool. Dust with icing sugar and singe the top with a blow torch, and allow to cool.

4. Put remaining sugar and blackberries into a pan on a gentle heat with two tablespoons water, stir frequently as the blackberries soften and sauce thickens. Add the brandy, stir and allow to cool.

5. Cut flan into eight equal wedges and dust with a little icing sugar, and serve with blackberry sauce.

Farmers' markets

Carmarthen
Town Centre
1st Friday each month
T: 01550 777244

Celyn Farmers Market
The Sports Hall, North Wales College
Horticulture, Northop
3rd Sunday each month
T: 01745 561999

Chepstow
Senior Citizens Centre
2nd, 3rd Saturday each month
T: 01291 650672

Colwyn Bay
Bay View Shopping
Centre car park
Each Thursday
T: 01492 680209

Conwy Country Market
Royal British Legion
Each Tuesday
T: 01492 592455

Cowbridge
Arthur Johns Car Park, High Street
1st & 3rd Saturday each month
T: 01656 661100

Dolgellau
Eldon Square
3rd Sunday each month
T: 01341 422808

Fishguard
Town Hall
Saturday each fortnight
T: 01348 873004

Haverfordwest
Riverside Shopping
Friday each fortnight
T: 01437 776168

**For up-to-date farmers markets
visit website www.fmiw.co.uk**

Aberaeron
Alban Square Field
(Inner Harbour)
1st Wednesday each month
(June – October)
T: 01970 633066

Abergavenny
Market Hall
4th Thurday each month
T: 01873 860271

Aberystwyth
North Parade
1st – 3rd Saturday
each month
T: 01970 633066

Brecon
Market Hall
2nd Saturday each month
T: 01874 636169

Caerphilly
Twyn Community Centre
2nd Saturday each month
T: 01656 658963

Cardigan
Upper Market Hall, Pendre
2nd Thursday each month
(May – September)
T: 01970 633066

Cardiff Riverside
Community Market
Fitzhammon Embankment,
Every Sunday
T: 029 2019 0036

Glasfryn Parc
Pwllheli
2nd Sunday each month
T: 01766 810044

Glyndwr
Station Campsite, Carrog, nr Corwen
1st Sunday each month
(May – October)
T: 01691 860357

Llanberis
Church Hall, Caernafon
1st Friday each month
T: 01286 870605

Knighton
Community Centre
2nd, 4th Saturday each month
T: 01547 520096

Lampeter
Market Street
Alternate Fridays
T: 01570 423200

Llandovery
Market Square
Last Saturday each month
T: 01550 720233

Llandrindod Wells
Middleton Street
Last Thursday each month
T: 01597 824102

Llandudno
Town Hall
2nd Friday each month

Llangefni, Anglesey
Thursday & Saturday
T: 01248 490578

Llangollen Market
Market Street
Every Tuesday

Llanrwst
Ancaster Square
3rd Saturday each month
T: 01492 651033

Llantrisant
Old Victorian School
2nd Friday each month
T: 01443 237774

Merthyr Tydfil
High Street
1st Friday each month
T: 01685 725106

Mold
St Marys Church Hall
1st Saturday each month
T: 01745 561999

Mumbles
Seafront, (Oystermouth) Car Park
2nd Saturday each month
T: 01792 405169

Newport
Bridge Street
2nd, 4th Friday each month
T: 01633 263117

Pembroke
Town Hall
Saturday fortnightly
T: 01646 680090

Penarth
Westbourne School, Penarth
4th Saturday each month
T: 01565 661100

Penclawdd Local Produce Market
Penclawdd Community Centre
3rd Saturday each month
T: 01792 850147

Penderyn Community Centre
Last Sunday each month
T: 01685 812545

Presteigne
Radnorshire Arms Hotel
1st Saturday each month

Porthcawl
Arwel-y-Mor Hall, Porthcawl
4th Saturday each month
T: 01656 058963

Port Talbot
Aberafan Shopping Centre
1st, 3rd Saturday each month
T: 01639 882274

Rhayader
2nd Thursday each month
T: 01597 810081

Ruthin Produce Market
Old Gaol Courtyard,
St Peters Sq
Last Saturday each month
(May – October)
T: 07798 914721

Sketty Produce Market
Sketty Parish Hall, St Pauls Church
1st Saturday each month
T: 01792 850162

Tonypandy
Dunraven Street
2nd Friday each month
T: 01443 425343

Usk
Memorial Hall
1st & 3rd Saturday each month
T: 0845 6106496

**Waterfront Local Produce Market
(Swansea)**
National Waterfront
Museum, Maritime Quarter, Swansea
1st Sunday each month

Welshpool Market
Town Hall
1st Friday
T: 01686 626606

Wrexham
Queen Square
3rd Friday each month
T: 01978 292010

Food festivals

March

Sundersfoot St David's Day
Saundersfoot Harbour
T: 01834 812304

April

Experience Wales Pavilion at the Royal Horticultural Society Spring Flower Show
Bute Park, Cardiff
T: 029 2087 3914

Mid-Wales Mouthful
Royal Welsh Showground,
Builth Wells
T: 01938 552224
www.wonderwoolwales.co.uk/
mouthful

Llanwrtyd Wells Gourmet Festival
Bromsgrove Hall & Fields, Llanwrtyd
Wells
T: 01591 610264
www.food-food-food.co.uk

May

Food Celebration
Swan Bank, Hay-on-Wye
T: 01479 820740
www.foodcelebration.co.uk

Pembroke Potato Festival
Pembroke town centre
T: 01646 680090

The Smallholders Show
Royal Welsh Showground, Built Wells
T: 01982 553683
www.rwas.co.uk

Welsh Perry & Cider Festival
Clytha Arms, near
Abergavenny
T: 01685 873866
www.welshcider.co.uk

June

Great Welsh Beer & Cider Festival
Cardiff city centre venue
T: 01792 514564

Hay-on-Wye Food Festival
Memorial Car Park, High Street,
Hay-on-Wye
T: 01874 624979

Llandysul Food Festival
Llandysul Park, Llandysul
T: 01559 362403

Llanerchaeron Brewing Weekend
Llanerchaeron, near
Aberaeron
T: 01545 573024

Llŷn Seafood Festival / Gwyl Fwyd Môr Llŷn
Pwllheli
T: 07890 036357

Pembrokeshire Fish Week
Various venues throughout
Pembrokeshire
T: 01437 776168
www.pembrokeshirefishweek.co.uk

The Welsh Game Fair
Gelli Aur, Llandeilo
T: 01267 281410
www.welshgamefair.com

July

Caerphilly Big Cheese Festival
Caerphilly Castle,
Caerphilly
T: 01496 235872
www.caerphilly.gov.uk/bigcheese

Cardiff International Food & Drink Festival
Roald Dahl Plass,
Cardiff Bay
T: 029 2087 3914
www.cardiff-festival.com

Cardigan Bay Seafood Festival
Aberaeron
T: 07880 727770 /
01545 570755

Get Welsh in Swansea
Castle Square, Swansea
T: 01792 514503

Lampeter Food Festival
University of Wales Lampeter
Campus, Lampeter
T: 01570 424704

The Royal Welsh Show
Royal Welsh Showground,
Builth Wells
T: 01982 553683
www.rwas.co.uk

August

The Big Welsh Bite
Ynysangharad
Memorial Park, Pontypridd
T: 01443 490200

Brecon Beacons Summer Fayre
National Park Visitor Centre,
Libanus, Brecon
T: 01874 624979
www.breconbeacons.org

Cardigan River & Food Festival
Quay Street/ Somerfield car park,
Cardigan
T: 01239 615554

Gwyl Fwyd A Chrefft Y Frenni
Crymych
T: 01239 831455

Pembrokeshire Agricultural Show
Withybush Showground,
Haverfordwest
T: 01437 764331
www.pembrokeshirecountyshow.co.uk

Really Wild Food & Countryside Festival
St David's Football Ground, St David's
T: 01348 840242
www.reallywildfestival.co.uk

The Welsh Food Festival
Glansevern Hall Gardens, Berriew
T: 01686 640916
www.welshfoodfestival.co.uk

September

Abergavenny Food Festival
Abergavenny town centre
T: 01873 851643
www.abergavennyfoodfestival.com

Aberystwyth Food & Drink Festival
Baker Street,
Aberystwyth
T: 01970 633066

Bridgend Festival of Wales
Bridgend town centre
T: 01656 661338

Harvest Fayre
Riverside Quay Shopping Centre,
Haverfordwest
T: 01437 776168
www.pembrokeshire.gov.uk/foodanddrink

Mold Food Festival
Mold town centre
T: 01352 758622
www.moldfoodfestival.co.uk

Narberth Food Festival
Queens Hall,
Narberth
T: 01834 860268
www.narberthfoodfestival,co,uk

October

Anglesey Oyster Festival
Trearddur Bay Hotel, Trearddur Bay,
Anglesey
T: 01248 725700
www.angleseyoysterfestival.com

Brecon Beacons Food Festival
Market Hall, Brecon
T: 01874 624979
www.breconbeacons.org

Cowbridge Food Festival
Various venues throughout
Cowbridge
T: 01446 773171
www.cowbridgefoodanddrink.org

Gwledd Conwy Feast
Conwy town centre
T: 01492 593874
www.conwyfoodfestival.co.uk

Llangollen Food Festival
International
Pavilion, Llangollen
T: 01824 705802
www.llangollenfoodfestival.co.uk

November

Wales Food Festival
Aberystwyth Arts Centre,
Aberystwyth
T: 01970 622889

Brecon Beacons Christmas Fayre
Memorial Car Park, Hay-on-Wye
T: 01874 624979
www.breconbeacons.org

Llandudno Celtic Winter Fayre
Mostyn Champneys, Llandudno
T: 01492 574524
www.celticwinterfayre.co.uk

Llandysul Christmas Fair
In and around
Llandysul
T: 01559 362403

December

Aberystwyth Christmas Food & Craft Fayre
Baker Street,
Aberyswyth
T: 01970 633066

Caerphilly Christmas Market
Caerphilly town centre
T: 01496 235872

Llanerchaeron Christmas Fair
Llanerchaeron, near
Aberaeron
T: 01545 573024

Index

S - Y